© Dr. Lisa Cook, LPC, CPC. Coming Out-How to Reclaim Your Power and Live Your Authentic Truth to Create Life Impact All Rights Reserved.

All rights reserved. No portion of this book may be reproduced in any form without permission from the publisher, except as permitted by U.S. copyright law. For permissions contact:

lifeimpactcircles@outlook.com

Life Impact Circles ~ Publisher

Editing: Jessica Gang

Book Cover: Eva Thomas

ISBN: 978-1-7345361-0-2

Dr. Lisa Cook, LPC, CPC

TABLE OF CONTENTS

BOOK DEDICATION V

ACKNOWLEDGMENTS VII

INTRODUCTION 1

SECTION ONE ~ REFLECTIVE & RETROSPECTIVE ANALYSIS . 9

CHAPTER 1 ....PURPOSEFUL REFLECTIVE & RETROSPECTIVE ANALYSIS ~ PEERING BACKWARDS IS NECESSARY TO COMING OUT!.. 10

CHAPTER 2......IDENTIFYING THE TRAUMATIC EVENTS & THE MEANING THAT WAS CREATED FOR YOU 20

PERSONAL COMING OUT JOURNEY WORK ~ REFLECTIVE & RETROSPECTIVE ANALYSIS ~ AWARENESS 29

SECTION 2 ~ RECONNECTING TO YOUR EMOTIONS ~ AWARENESS.. 33

CHAPTER 3.....................EXAMINE THE EMOTIONS AND COPING BEHAVIORS FORMED 34

CHAPTER 4..FIGHTING FOR YOU IS PARAMOUNT!.. 47

PERSONAL COMING OUT JOURNEY WORK ~ RECONNECTING TO YOUR EMOTIONS ~ AWARENESS 53

SECTION 3 ~ RECOGNITION OF THE POWER OF YOUR VOICE AND STRENGTH ~ ACKNOWLEDGEMENT 59

CHAPTER 5 .... COMING OUT COMMENCES ~ ACKNOWLEDGEMENT & ACCEPTANCE PRINCIPLE 60

CHAPTER 6 .... COMING OUT OF SHAME & VICTIM MENTALITY 68

CHAPTER 7 .... COMING OUT OF GUILT & NON-FORGIVENESS 82

CHAPTER 8 .... COMING OUT OF UNHEALTHY RELATIONSHIPS 88

CHAPTER 9 ....
COMING OUT ANGER 97

PERSONAL COMING OUT JOURNEY WORK ~ RECOGNITION OF THE POWER OF YOUR VOICE AND STRENGTH ~ ACKNOWLEDGEMENT 107

SECTION 4 ~ RECLAIM YOUR AUTHENTIC VOICE & PERSONAL POWER FOR POSITIVE & HEALTHY WAYS OF LIVING ~ ACCEPTANCE 119

CHAPTER 10 .... COMING TO SELF LOVE & SELF ACCEPTANCE 120

PERSONAL COMING OUT JOURNEY WORK ~ RECLAIM YOUR AUTHENTIC VOICE & PERSONAL POWER FOR POSITIVE & HEALTHY WAYS OF LIVING ~ ACKNOWLEDGEMENT 129

SECTION 5 ~ RENOVATE YOUR PERSONAL LIFE VISION BY FORWARD MOVEMENT ~ ACTION 132

CHAPTER 11 .... COMING OUT AND COMING TO IS LIFELONG 133

CHAPTER 12 .... CASTING A VISION TO CATAPULT YOUR FORWARD MOVEMENT 139

QUOTES TO INFLUENCE CHANGE 146

REFERENCES..148
INDEX..151
ABOUT THE AUTHOR..153

Book Dedication

This book is dedicated to my daughter, Cieyara, who is a gift from God that I was not always able to honor due to my past trauma. I'm so grateful for her perseverance, tenacity, strength, and courage which allowed me to see the beauty of her being my child and the beauty of her being herself. Ultimately, her love pushed me beyond the dysfunction to seek a more functional way of living. For many years, I was blind to the exceptionalism of her being because I could only see her through *my* lens of unworthiness, shame, and lack of value. Her unrelenting love, integrity, and authenticity to herself knocked down every trammel that I placed in front of her to push me to this moment. Thank you, Brown! You are a remarkable creation and purposed by God to leave a lasting impact on all you intersect with in this life. I love you with every breath of my being and to the moon and beyond!

With Love,
Mom

Dr. Lisa Cook, LPC, CPC

Acknowledgements

Special thanks to the individuals whose lives I have crossed in this journey that inspired me either by mistreatment or by encouragement. God has allowed each experience to influence my power and push me forward. A special gratitude to my mom, who instilled faith in her children, and gave her all to her life and to her family! Thank you to Cedric Johnson, who told me to never lie to myself! Thank you to the individuals who remained true and shared their humanity with me, you have already created life impact in my life.

To You (the Reader)

It is very important as you read my *Coming Out* truth that you do not view me as a victim. For years, I wore that title and now I have thrown it away. Victims do not ask for their attacks or assaults, but they can live a life that produces more victimization if there is not a conscious pursuit to change their internal script, which plays in one's mind each day.

Introduction

One early morning, as I read my journals spanning over seventeen years, I began to recognize a pulsing intensity in my chest and a lump emerging in my throat. I asked myself, "What could be the cause of this physical manifestation within my body and the tears rolling down my face?" It is my belief that my physical reaction was an outward expression of the intersection of my reflective writings about my life with my truth finally exclaiming to my heart, "It is time to come out!"

Hearing the common vernacular such as, *Coming Out* may allow one's mind to conjure that this book is about coming out of the closet and telling the world about one's sexuality, but that is not what the phrase *Coming Out* means for me. I am referring to the years of hiding behind a family name, a family image, and covering up personal insecurities and personal failures. Mostly, I am referencing a lifetime of pain, anger, and learned destructive and manipulative cognitions and behaviors that framed my life. I am referencing the illogical thinking patterns and self-defeating coping mechanisms formed from childhood sexual abuse, emotional neglect, and abandonment. Additionally, I am including the self-sabotage patterns that allowed me to sacrifice my own honor and worth as a woman within the context of my family, my motherhood, and my womanhood. I classify this common vernacular *Coming Out* to mean the exercise that one completes to honor oneself, to honor one's values, and to honor his/her own voice with the objective to transform one's personal life using the true power that each individual holds within their possession. Ultimately, the energy created in the *Coming Out* process can permeate outwardly and transcend to others within each person's life intersections.

In my life, I have always loved one particular animal. My attraction to this animal originated from what this animal seems to represent to me. It represents freedom, forward movement, and having free reign to maneuver one's self. It may surprise many that this animal is the zebra. Whenever I observed zebras on television as a young girl, I noticed that they ran in a pack going forward, and the way the zebras ran seemed to be so free and with such ease. The symbolism of the zebras running so gracefully spoke to my hidden side. The parts of myself that many people in my life did not see. This hidden side of myself aligned with the symbolism of the running zebras, which represented my ability to run from the very thing I needed to face. The fundamental question was, "What did I need to face in my life?"

Truthfully, I have been running all my life … running from and looking for… What was I running from or looking for? I was looking for someone to catch me, to save me, or to fight for me. Now, the imagery of the zebra running represents two aspects for me in my *Coming Out* experience. One aspect is me running from myself in a self-neglectful way and the other aspect is me running to myself in a loving and healthy way.

Over the last four years, my life circumstances shifted in such painful and traumatic ways. It forced me to halt the running and face all the unpleasant experiences that shaped my life. In the process of recovery, I chose to write my *Coming Out* story in order to tell my truth, to honor my voice, and release the personal power to transition my life to a healthier space. I hope that my vulnerabilities will inspire others to come out to honor their voices, and toil through the internal resistance to move forward to a healthier life and relationships.

Coming Out!

Honor and Value Your Personal Voice

I possess a personal philosophy that each of us must honor and value our authentic voice, which may have been lost or misplaced through life's traumas or circumstances, to become our truest and best selves!

The demonstration of honoring and valuing your voice equates to not giving in to what others say you should be in this world. To the contrary, it recognizes the voice that cries out for you to be who God created you to be or live within the purpose of your creation. Each of us has a spiritual and physical purpose to make life impact!

Honor, Value, and Life Impact are three important concepts for us to strive for in our daily lives. We all have value, we all have honor, and we all have life impact, but these areas can be stifled from unawareness of who we are authentically and our power to make measurable adjustment in our lives. For some of us, the exercise of *Coming Out* of the negative internal scripts that directed our lives can shift us to more positive, healthier, and functional living! Essentially, each of us have a chance to evolve, but it is solely within each individual's prerogative to make that choice!

In addition, I believe that each person's individual mantra could be: "I will allow myself permission to rediscover and recognize the value of my authentic voice and I will choose to live a lifestyle that honors my person." Taking steps to unleash the personal power within can bring significant impact to your life and spills outward to all who intersect with your truest self.

According to the Merriam Webster Dictionary the word "value" means to have "relative worth, utility, or importance; something (such as principle or quality) intrinsically valuable or desirable." [12] Additionally, Merriam Webster Dictionary defines the word "honor" to have "a keen sense of ethical conduct: integrity, one whose worth brings respect." [11]

Life impact occurs whether constituted as big or small, minute or massive, when one chooses to value and honor their selves and their purpose. The fundamental question for each of us remains, *"What do I want my life impact to be?"*

The Process

This book will focus on the *"Four-A's Principle"* – *"Awareness, Acknowledgment, Acceptance, and Action"* as well as outline a practical process to *Coming Out* with the goal of honoring, valuing, and creating life impact via one's authentic voice to Connect to a Better, Stronger You!

The *Coming Out* process will include the following steps:

Reflective and Retrospective Analysis. This exercise is central to the *Coming Out* experience. It leads to an internal and historical research of yourself via asking and answering the tough questions, categorizing the themes of the answers, and identifying the trauma events from your past, along with the meaning that those events created in your life. *~Awareness*

Reconnecting with Your Emotions. This exercise is important, as this is the space where your avoided or denied emotions are actualized. Additionally, this experience creates movement for you to permit yourself to travel beyond the emotional pillars you may have created.

Awareness and Acknowledgment

Recognition of the Power of Your Voice and Strength. This lifelong exercise is a vital recognition and reality to live in, in order to shift your life forward in positive and healthy ways. *~Acknowledgment*

Reclaim your Authentic Voice and Personal Power for Positive and Healthy Ways of Living. This is important to initiating the forgiveness process of the meaning and events in your past experiences and re-esteeming yourself. ~*Acceptance*

Renovate your Personal Life Vision and Pursue Forward Movement. This space is about your drive for transformation. It starts with the creation of your future with a personal mantra and a vision, inclusive of your readiness for forward movement to functional and healthy life experiences. ~ *Action*

The Four-A's Principle

Awareness is being willing to see the truth about you and your life. *Acknowledgment* is being willing to tell yourself the truth. *Acceptance* is being willing to live the truth and choose a new way. *Action* is being willing to take what you have learned and know about this truth, then go forward into a better, stronger version of yourself.

My development of *The Four-A's Principle* commenced from my experience with the commonly known "Serenity Prayer," which reads as "God grant me the serenity to accept the things that we cannot change, the courage to change the things that we can and wisdom to know the difference." [1] No one really knows the original author and this prayer is highly associated with the recovery movement. However, I found that this prayer is more than a recitation of words, but is a basis for a personal, internal transformation that produces external physiological, cognitive, and emotional results in my life.

In digging deeper into the words of the serenity prayer, I found the meaning of the words holding great promise for my growth. Let us break down this prayer:

Serenity – "a state of being calm, peaceful and untroubled." [5]

Acceptance – "the action of consisting to receive or undertake something offered." [5]

Courage – "the ability to do something that frightens one." [5]

Wisdom – "the quality of having experience, knowledge and good judgment." [5]

Awareness – Being Willing to See the Truth

In this life, each person has the potential to carry parts of their life history with them that they do not want to deal with nor face. Some of our life histories are extremely painful and some of them have been pushed into the recesses of our mind. Some of our life histories are embarrassing to us, or may have damaged our self-image or self-esteem, and we have determined that we want to keep the past in the past. Yet, we have some wonderful memories of our past as well. *Awareness* becomes a part of our *Coming Out* journey when we come to a place where we seek a calming, peaceful and untroubled existence, in essence, we want serenity. We have an unspoken yearning or alarming cry that sounds off when something in our life or in us is counter-balanced with who we say we are or how we are living our life. Whether by external forces or internal consciousness, we must come to a point where we are willing to tell ourselves the truth! This is the birth of our awareness for growth! You become willing to make this request, "God grant me the peace I need to see the truth about myself, not necessarily without fear, but with courage."

Acknowledgement – Being Willing to Tell Yourself the Truth

My significant other once told me that I should never lie to myself. I found his simple statement to be so profound, especially as we understand our acknowledgment practice. A state of calm and peacefulness is rewarded to us by God when there is acknowledgment of who you are and awareness of the historical imprint that defines your personality, your thoughts, your drive, and the person you are today. As you begin to see the truth, you come to the realization that the energy you exerted not facing the truth can be the same energy you transfer into your willingness to acknowledge the truth that is currently being revealed to you. The fear that possessed you and that you allowed to rule your thinking, can be diminished when you acknowledge the offering of a gift of peace. The exact moment that you acknowledge this gift of peace, is the exact moment your power of personal choice and transformation begin to honor you. This simple act of willingness to acknowledge yourself is powerful and is the portal to tell yourself the truth. As you experience the ability to see the truth about yourself, you now start to visualize your strength to courageously move forward toward gaining wisdom about your life, despite any lingering self-judgment, negative thinking, or arrogant cognitive processing.

Acceptance – Being Willing to Live the Truth and Choose a New Way.

In the process of awareness and acknowledgment, one of the biggest acts of courage will be your acceptance of what you now see in yourself. It could look completely different because the blinders and barriers you instituted are starting to erode. Your vision of yourself should be becoming clearer. In this point of *Coming Out*, you recognize that another necessary action of acceptance is your self-love. Pulling back the curtain, coming out raw and unrefined, seeing your vulnerabilities and your needs must be accepted. Strength lies in our personal acceptance and our courage will fuel the intrinsic power to make another choice to move forward. Here is where the wisdom of the serenity prayer makes sense.

You are learning about yourself; you are accepting yourself, and now you have more knowledge of what worked and what can be corrected by you.

Action – Being Willing to Take What You Have Learned and Know About This Truth

Wisdom from a biblical perspective indicates that you use your knowledge to make a better choice. The goal is not to just know something, but to do something different or to adjust ourselves based on this attained knowledge. Here, you are the center of that goal, which requires exerted energy! It is internal and external energy to bring to fruition the truth into a better choice for you, and then go forward into a better, stronger version of yourself. Action is intentional and consistent with a daily discipline to gain ground on your default behavior. Default programming is the thinking and the behaviors you have been operating from before you started your self-awareness journey and this *Coming Out* process requires learning new skills.

In my journey of *Coming Out*, I was able to quantify my experience into *The Four-A's Principle*. This principle can be easily applied to your life as you seek personal growth toward living out of your authentic voice to honor and value yourself.

Section 1
Reflective and Retrospective Analysis ~ Awareness

1

Purposeful Reflective and Retrospective Analysis ~ Peering Backward is Necessary to Coming Out!

"**P**urposeful" is defined by the Merriam Webster Online Dictionary as an adjective with the following meaning: 1) having a purpose: such as a) meaningful or b) intentional or 2) full of determination. [9]

In the consideration of the *Coming Out* process, there must be an understanding that you will look backward to discover how the past has shaped you in the present. Additionally, with the goal of using this understanding to make a meaningful shift in your life's direction. Purposefully looking backward should provide a space to engage the emotions or feelings that you may have displaced due to your experiences. Furthermore, it

> It begins with you making the choice to dedicate time for you and your individualized growth.

helps to identify what events, experiences, or messages that hold you hostage, causing you to not make personal progress.

It begins with you making the choice to dedicate time for you and your individualized growth. It will be necessary to be intentional with your heart, your soul, and your mind. You will allow yourself permission to embark on your reflective look internally and your retrospective look historically for your life.

It is as simple and fearful as asking yourself this question: "Is there any credence or any truth to what I'm hearing about my character or behavior?' Over the course of your life, there have been moments when someone mentioned to you or made a comment about something that you did or said. Typically, if what was stated hit home, you probably rejected it.

For instance, I recall after splitting from my ex-husband and having a conversation with my mom and her friend Mr. James where I was blaming my-ex-husband for the failure of our marriage. Mr. James posed a question to me, which was: "Did you ever think the problem was you?" I immediately stated, "No!" However, in contemplation I wondered if I could have been the problem? I quickly answered myself, stating internally that he was the one with the addiction issues. I was not even close to being ready to see that Mr. James was not blaming me for my ex-husband's behavior in the marriage but he was asking me to stop blaming him and seeking victim status. I needed to look within to ask myself the tough questions that lead me to the relationship in the first place.

That conversation was over twenty years ago but it continually popped up in my mind like a flashing yellow light seeking my attention and telling me to slow down and understand its meaning for my own personal growth.

Another recent situation that may seem common to many parents is hearing these words, "You don't care!" These are the words that are spoken, yelled, and believed by my teenage daughter. My initial reaction to those words was always combative, meaning I rejected it in every way, and I was unwilling to ask myself the tough question about this recurring commentary from my daughter.

As we all seek fulfilled and functional lives, we must really ask ourselves how authentic we are to ourselves and to others. I firmly believe that our lives only shift toward fulfillment and functionality when there is honesty internally and we are not afraid to be ourselves and we make the efforts to see the truth about ourselves.

The internal reflective and historical retrospective analysis of our lives will help us begin the process of discovering the emotional pillars preventing growth, authenticity, and functionality in our lives.

What Are the Questions We Should Ask Ourselves?

I would argue some of our best questions come at the pinnacle of our most painful moments. After my separation to my addictive ex-husband, I remember sitting at my desk at work crying because I was in so much pain from the marriage ending and my discovery that my husband was the epitome of everything I vowed not to marry based on my childhood. I began questioning myself: I asked myself questions such as:

How did I get here?
How come I did not see the signs of his addiction?
What was it about me that attracted this type of relationship?
Was my marriage an attempt to meet the criteria of what I measured as having success in life?

Coming Out!

Did I marry to be accepted or have more value in my family or my community?

Or, when I sat in my quiet moments after a poorly communicated, anxiety-ridden, and traumatic episode that I manifested with my daughter, I would ask myself questions such as:

Why does she believe that I don't care about her?
Am I really paying attention to what matters to her or to what matters to me?
As a parent who loves my daughter, why am I manifesting energy into our relationship that tells her that I don't care?
Why did I continually create these chaotic episodes for my daughter?

Most recently, I experienced the most significant pain of my life that involved my family and shook the core of my spiritual and family foundation. Again, this experience propelled me to those reflective and retrospective questions, here are a few of them:
Why was I susceptible to the deceit and manipulation of this religious community?
Why did I commit so much of my time and energy to an environment that I observed there was a duality of character?
What was the personal gain?

Once you are able to write these questions, then it is critically important to take the next step and answer them. Answering the questions leads to you discovering the emotional pillars that are holding you back or causing you to repeat patterns in your life. Either way, the patterns interfere with the functioning of your authentic self.

Answers to My Marriage Questions:

Q: How did I get here?
A: I chose to marry a man that I ignored his propensity for drinking and drugs. I also chose a man who was similar to the father figure of my childhood, who was an alcoholic, so I could perpetuate the same life patterns in my adulthood.

Q: How come I did not see the signs of his addiction?
A: I did not want to and denied them because I did not want to be alone.

Q: What was it about me that attracted this type of relationship?
A: I was attracted to chaos and dysfunction much like my childhood. I did not know that my internal script stated to me that this is what I need and deserve because I grew up in an alcoholic home. Additionally, I was not aware of my lack of self-identity and esteem.

Q: Was my marriage an attempt to meet the criteria of what I measured as having success in life?
A: Yes, I observed my older siblings' marriages and I saw that being married brought a level of esteem within the church and black community. I desperately sought after this esteem due to my lack of esteem.

Q: Did I marry to be accepted or have more value in my family or community?
A: Yes, I always wanted legitimacy with my family and to be seen as an equal or important to them.

Coming Out!

Answers to my Spiritual and Family Situation:

Q: Why was I susceptible to the deceit and manipulation of this religious community?

A: Due to my childhood sexual abuse and the messages that I believed about myself, my vulnerability was based on those experiences in my life. A part of me became unconsciously conditioned by deceit due to carrying the belief that I contributed to my childhood abuse by not communicating what happened to me.

Q: Why did I commit so much of my time and energy to an environment that I observed there was a duality of character (good and bad)?

A: I lived my life with dualities because my home life was good at times, but then riddled by my oldest alcoholic brother that created great chaos and stress in my life. However, when I presented myself to the world, I pretended that my home life was perfect and that I did not have any problems. Entering a church environment that I saw people on Sundays as holy rollers and then on Sunday afternoon through Saturday as heathens became almost normative. I was very susceptible to the cultish manipulation of the church because of my strong need for validity and acceptance. Further, I would rationalize against my spirit and did not trust myself to follow my inner voice to vacate this environment.

Q: What was the personal gain?

A: I got value from the work I did in the religious community. I was good at it, which resulted in much praise and acceptance for me. Additionally, I finally seemed to be able to have value in my family as I became more prominent in my church community. Also, I personally believed that raising my daughter in the religious community and teaching her biblical principles was the right thing to do. My internal thinking regarding my daughter was for her to be the person that I was not ... perfect and acceptable to my family and to the world because I believed that I had no self-worth and I could not accept myself based on my abuse and past.

Answers to My Questions Related to My Daughter:

Q: Why does she believe that I don't care about her?
A: I was making choices that put my needs over her needs and I could not see that.

Q: Am I really paying attention to what matters to her or to what matters to me?
A: I convinced myself that her needs would be met, if my needs were satisfied.

Q: As a parent who loves my daughter, why am I manifesting energy into our relationship that tells her that I don't care?
A: Truth was ... that I did not listen to her needs and because I only believed myself as being able to fulfill certain needs, I rejected all requests for me to reach inside myself to be different and have more compassion for someone else's needs. I was void of compassion because I was wired with the strength to survive, not the strength to be soft, caring, and compassionate emotionally.

Q: Why did I continually create these chaotic episodes for my daughter?

A: This chaotic dynamic was all I knew, and it reflected what I thought family life was supposed to be. Thus, I recreated the dysfunctional dynamic that feeds all of my unhealthy vices.

Once you are able to honestly answer your tough questions, go a step further and try to identify the themes. Identify the words that have meaning for you or the repeated words/phrases found in your answers. Again, these are clues in your discovery or identification of those emotional pillars that are present in your life and impeding your forward movement.

You can document your themes/repeated words in various ways, but it can look like the example below:

Situations	Repeated Words/Themes
Marriage Dissolution	Childhood, alcoholic, denial, chaos/dysfunction, level of esteem, legitimacy with family, seen as equal in my family
Religious/Family	Childhood sexual abuse, I contributed to abuse, dualities/pretended, alcoholic, praise/acceptance, value in my family, perfect/acceptable daughter
Mother/Daughter Relationship	My needs over her needs, listening to her needs, void of compassion, strength to survive

Painful moments were the catalyst to answering the questions to gain awareness from these particular situations in my life. This process taught me if I participated in reflective and retrospective analysis regularly, I would discover a great deal about myself. Instead, of avoiding my needs, querying myself about my intentions produces greater self-authenticity.

With the goal being how to work to be functional and authentic in healthier ways in our lives, we must come to accept that the practice of reflective and retrospective analysis is a lifelong exercise. Your awareness can continue to strengthen, as the future exercises may not focus so much on pain, but on maintaining progress of transformation and forward movement.

After you have asked the tough questions and highlighted the themes within your answers, the next transition is to determine the meaning for your life and greater self-awareness.

What Do Your Themes Tell You About Your Life?

My reflective internal analysis and retrospective historical analysis evidenced that my abuse and its aftermath was ruling my life. The chaotic propensity for my relationships was deeply rooted in my psyche and spirit. My energy sought to live in this dysfunction in most aspects of my life. Duality was normative, despite the damage it was rendering in my life. Most astounding there was a severe lack of esteem and self-acceptance which propelled many of my choices that were unconsciously detrimental to my life and my daughter.

Here is the deal! Was it my fault that I had created this type of life for myself? No, it was due to a lack of awareness and doing the best that I could with the tools I possessed for this life. Out of blindness, we can morph into many things that are far away from whom we were created to be in this world.

Our lives only shift toward fulfillment and functionality when there is honesty internally and we are not afraid to be ourselves and we make the efforts to see the truth about ourselves.

2

Identifying the Traumatic Events and Meaning That Was Created for You

I grew up in a family of twelve siblings with what I would describe as an older set of siblings and a younger set of siblings. My position in the family is the youngest. My childhood memories are marked by wonderful fun times with my siblings, nieces, nephews, and cousins. Additionally, those years were etched into my psyche by trauma. It was the trauma of growing up with an alcoholic older brother who often terrorized our household when he was intoxicated. I distinctly remember the smell of gin permeating through the home and one of the Temptations' favorites blaring, "Papa Was a Rolling Stone." If this song was playing, this was an indication of a night of harassment and chaos by my older brother. This recurring episode

> **Painful moments were the catalyst to answering the questions to gain awareness from these particular situations in my life.**

happened monthly when he would get his social security benefits for his disability, and I dreaded this time of month. There were times that I recall hiding under the bed, placing the blankets over me so it appeared I was not there, hiding in my mother's closet whenever I knew his presence was approaching the area that I was in. This unspoken fear rode upon my sub-conscious for a long period of my life. I believed that it sparked the beginning of the hyper-vigilance that I experienced for the majority of my life.

My pre-adolescence and teen years were filled with the love of sports, primarily basketball for me, and I would go on to play collegiate basketball on sports scholarships. I became very independent in my teen years and spent the majority of my time away from home. As I looked back on my life, I found that my pre-adolescence and teen years were also marked with three traumatic episodes that shaped my thinking and resiliency. However, I never learned how to cope effectively or process any emotions that were associated with these life altering periods; therefore, I repeated the patterns of dysfunction into my adult life and into my parenting.

During my formative years, I grew up in a small rural, predominantly Caucasian town in the Midwest. This town had state facilities like a developmental center and two state prisons that employed many persons that came from the city of Chicago or other surrounding cities. My mom worked at the developmental center and this was a substantial employment for our family. We moved from Chicago to this small town as a better opportunity for our family, which included a different environment and sport opportunities. My family held a significant prominence because of my siblings and my success with sports. So despite the chaos inside my family home, when we stepped outside of the doors of our home, we projected an image of family pride and that all things were perfect. We never spoke about the issues within our home to outsiders.

Let me be clear, there is absolutely nothing wrong with reflecting pride in your family or choosing not to share your life story with every person you meet in your life.

There are probably many reasons for this dynamic, including: 1) culturally and generationally African American families always stood proud while intersecting with the Caucasian community; and 2) African American families historically do not share family secrets and are very protective of the family name.

I share this insight about my family because it subconsciously impacted me. As the duality of my family life and non-family life led to my dysfunction and my esteem challenges.

The Abuse

When I was around the age of eleven or twelve, I was sexually assaulted by my brother-in-law and his twin brother the first summer I went to stay with my sister. He would come to the living room where I slept each night and fondle me repeatedly while I laid on the couch in Milwaukee. I did not understand what was going on when these events would occur during the nighttime. Then there was one day when my sister was gone that her husband and his twin brother tied me down to a bed and forced themselves on me. I recall being terrified and feeling like there was no escape from this situation. My recollection revealed seeing myself (a young girl) there in this bed laying lifeless and never crying a single tear as I separated myself from my emotions

> **My emotions were lost in the abyss of captivity to this trauma.**

that very second, that very moment, and that very day. My emotions were lost in the abyss of captivity to this trauma. I would not become aware that I needed to cry for the little girl until years later during my *Coming Out* process.

The second summer, as a teenager, her husband would take me out of his own daughter's bed with my sister upstairs and have sex with me repeatedly, raping me ... because I never told him that he could have sex with me or violate me. I never shared these experiences with my family until I was an adult.

In my late twenties, I suffered from recurring flashbacks during sleep. These dreams always consisted of a man chasing me, sometimes the man was identifiable and other times that man was not. These dreams became more intense and vivid when I was pregnant with my daughter, which caused me to pursue therapy. The dreams would always have a man or men who would have his genitals exposed while in pursuit of me. Further, I would run and try to find hiding spaces, so that I could not get caught. If I was ever caught in my dreams, I would try to find a way to hurt the man or men in a violent manner. In therapy, I started to recall memories of sexually abuse in my early childhood as well, but I spent the majority of my life without ever speaking a word of any of my abuse history. The seat of anger, rage, and disassociation to emotions originated from these experiences.

The Foster Home

During the second semester of my eighth grade year, I was taken from my family home and placed in a foster home. This foster home placement was not because I was a wayward kid, but because it was during a period of time that my older and closest sister disappeared and was reporting her childhood experience to the family. I remember distinctly receiving a phone call from her where she told me that she notified the police about my oldest brother's drinking and when they come to talk to me that I should tell the truth. One afternoon while I was in my eighth grade homeroom, I was called into the principal's office. As I entered the principal's office, there sat the police officers and they began to ask me questions about my home. I proceeded to share with them about my oldest brother's drinking. As I recall this experience, I think I secretly believed they would take my brother out of the home, but little did I know that I would be removed from the home. My mom was seeking to find my sister who had disappeared. My two older siblings and I were still at the home with my oldest brother during that time. The police officers and child protection services made the decision to take me to a foster home, so they escorted me home to get some belongings and took me to a foster home. I was in the foster home for two weeks before anyone in my family found me or called me. I was terrified and alone, but I did not express any of these emotions to anyone. I remained in the foster home the majority of my eighth grade year without approval for visitation with my family home because my brother lived in the home. I was so desperate to see my family that I would sneak over to my home during the day while telling the foster parents that I was going somewhere else.

It was my understanding that the child welfare personnel communicated that in order for me to return home my oldest brother would have to leave the home. My mother would have to make the choice for him to move out, so I could return home. However, to this present day, I am unaware of what the child welfare personnel communicated to my mom. At some point, I told myself internally without a conscious declaration that I wanted to go home by any means. Finally, when the court hearing arrived for me to testify against my brother, I recanted my entire story so I could go home. I made a sacrifice of my integrity at this young age to be with my family.

> **I made a sacrifice of my integrity at this young age to be with my family.**

The Death of My Sister

When I was a junior in high school, I was sitting with some of my college friends in their dorm room when my brother came to get me. Once I was with him, he told me that my favorite and closest older sister died. I recall feeling numb and not truly understanding what happened to her. The story that was shared with me was that she had not been seen coming out of her apartment for several days (her apartment was the basement apartment of my mom's apartment building in Chicago) and my mom went up to Chicago to see if she was okay. My mom entered her apartment and found her in a kneeling praying position in the bedroom, not breathing. There had to be a closed casket for her funeral because of her body's decompensation. I don't recall processing her loss and what her death meant to me.

Why is it valuable to identify the events or experiences from your past that could be hindering your present?

It is my belief that we are each being shaped every day by our life experiences and how we make meaning of those experiences. Whether it is in our childhood, teen years, young adult, or adulthood, there have been events that have shifted us in a direction to fulfill all of ourselves or to fulfill parts of ourselves.

My past experiences were heavily influential on the path I took in life, some of it was unconsciously driving me forward and some of it was a very conscious choice.

So, after you have completed these steps, the question becomes: Now what?

It is now time to figure out what meaning you associated with your life, your thinking, your soul, your heart, your relationships, your parenting, your work, your leisure, your drive, your pursuits, everything associated with you. How did these experiences and emotional pillars stand in the way or stop you from getting to know who you really are, or who you were destined and purposed to be?

The Meaning ~ What Internal Messages Did These Experiences Etch in My Psyche?

The Abuse

Growing up without a father in my life, these experiences created a lifelong fantasy of wanting a relationship with my father so he could be my protector. I longed for someone to protect me and often created pseudo-protection relationships with men where I thought I would get this need met.

I developed the thinking that men loved me only for my body (sex) and this was my only means to intimacy. I could easily dissociate my sexual experiences from my life as I did in the abuse situations. I carried shame and an unspoken hatred and disrespect for men. At the same time, these experiences told me to allow men to have power over me, even if it was hurtful to me. I lost trust in my own instincts and when men displayed interest in me, I could easily be manipulated by them.

I carried the message that I was not worthy of respect, nor did I really value, honor, or respect myself after these abusive experiences. Finally, for many years after the abuse, the experience fed a message to me to keep silent and not to tell my truth or my pain. Further, that my pain and my truth had no value and these elements could be sacrificed for the pleasure of someone else or the comfortability of others. In my *Coming Out* process, I discovered that my agreement with myself to remain silent and my self-sacrifice was one of the seeds to my anger and rage. Often times our families ask us to remain silent or sacrifice our truth without a spoken request…the request is rooted in our family culture and family dynamics.

The Foster Home

This experience made it perfectly clear to me at thirteen years of age that I must sacrifice my needs and my integrity to have my family. This theme permeated through my psyche my entire life where I gave myself whenever my family needed me, so I would not lose them. It seemed to be my only value to my family, or it was how I found value in my family.

I am not sure people can completely comprehend the feelings of insecurity and the fear that a thirteen-year-old takes on when taken from their family, placed in a foster home, and ordered by the court to have no contact with them unless supervised by court officials. While my family had issues as most families, it was my normalcy, so losing them or the threat of losing them was detrimental to me.

However, the choice that my mother made to not remove my brother so I could come home sent a message to my heart that I did not fully understand until Thanksgiving of 2015. Her choice told me that I was not worth fighting for, I was not good enough, and that I was loved less than my brother. This may not be true from her perspective, but it is the message that I received based on her decision. As a mother today, I can appreciate that she was in a difficult position and could not fully fathom how her choices would impact my life.

Dr. Lisa Cook, LPC, CPC

The Death of My Sister

All of my childhood memories of my sister conjure up a smile on my face and populate pleasant images in my mind. I distinctly recall her presence during the holiday season when she would come to the family home. She took remarkable details to everything from the fruit on the tables to the wrapping of the Christmas presents. Her entire presence set the ambience of our home, which brought such delight to me.

Our relationship was so special to me because when I was with her, I felt loved and cared for, and I knew I was important to her. I felt closer to her emotionally than anyone else in my family, so her death sent the message to me that the one person I believed truly loved me and could fight for me was gone and I was on my own.

Without taking the time to stop my pattern of running and facing myself, I would have never discovered I did not know *myself* or love *myself*. Nor would I have discovered that I did not like who I was, as I was living as a pretender. Taking the time to stop the pattern, allowed me to visualize that I was exposing to the world a pseudo-strong, accomplished, and poised African-American woman. However, I was also a young girl, afraid, without esteem, whom lacked emotional nurturing. I was angry and hardened. I punished myself daily as well as anyone who dared to come close enough to love me. I did not know that I was a people pleaser, doing for others so they could give me what I longed for … love, nurturing, protection, care, concern, and acceptance.

I had to look in the mirror and really see ME, Lisa, and realize that I could CATCH myself from falling … starting with awareness and telling myself the truth!

Personal Coming Out Journey Work
Reflective and Retrospective Analysis ~ Awareness

At this point, if you are ready to take a reflective and retrospective analysis of your life's traumatic events, here are some steps to initiate the process. *Please note: if you feel that you need the support of a therapist, a life coach, a spiritual coach, or trusted friend, do not hesitate to share with them and request their support.

~ Are you ready to make a choice for your individualized growth?

If so, can you give yourself intentional and dedicated time to work through the Awareness phase with an internal Reflective and historical Retrospective Analysis?

Is there any credence or any truth to what you have heard about your character or behavior? Any patterns of behavior that you do not understand?

If there are any pain points for you, what are the tough questions you must ask yourself? The personal questions should be specific to the situation.

~ How did I get here?
~ Why is the other person continually noting this behavior in me?
~ What is happening in my world when I am experiencing this?
~ What events from the past continue to recur for you in your dreams, thoughts, daydreams, and/or conversations?

After writing down your questions, take the time to answer them. *Answering the tough questions may take time. You should move at a pace comfortable for you, your physical, emotional, and mental health.

Next, try to document your themes or repeated words.

Situations	Repeated Words or Themes

If you able to identify these events, would you classify them as being traumatic or life impacting?

Merriam Webster defines "trauma" as "agent, force, or mechanism that causes trauma; an emotional upset; or a disordered psychic or behavioral state resulting from severe mental or emotional stress or physical injury." [8]

- ~ Notate these experiences the best you can, similar to how I have outlined my traumatic events.
- ~ Record the meanings that you have created based on these experiences by asking questions such as:
- ~ What do I tell myself based on this experience?
- ~ Can I see any of these messages emerge in other areas of my life based on this experience?
- ~ Can I identify if my choices are driven from this message(s)?
- ~ How have I navigated my life based on the messages I believe from my past experiences?

*You may feel raw or exposed, but please remember that this is the Awareness phase – Please tell yourself the truth! It will be uncomfortable, and your default programming and behavior will want to take over, but it is up to you to remember the choice you made for yourself to grow.

Section 2
Reconnecting with Your Emotions ~ Awareness

3

Examine the Emotions and Coping Behaviors Formed

Does this sound familiar?
Someone says a word or statement and your reaction is to immediately get emotionally elevated and verbally attack that person because this comment made you feel negative emotions from past events. Or, you respond with anger when someone violates a boundary and you express to that person how their actions offended you. Which one are you?

It is important to revisit the pain associated with your past experiences. This type of exercise assists you in unlocking blocked emotions, which will allow you to do the following:

a) Reconnect with your emotions in order to feel again.

b) Release the impact those experiences may have had on your physical body and

The goal for emotional healthiness is to experience our emotions and align our emotions accurately to the present-day experience.

mental self, inclusive of being present with those emotions.

c) Recognize the power you possess to relinquish your former identity as a victim by sharing your truth, expelling the negative energies outward from your spirit, and shifting your internal script with truthful mental reframes.

While you are re-connecting to emotions, it is important to mindful of emotions that you may have denied, and where you may have learned to be emotionally repressive. It is not healthy to replay the emotions associated to negative past experiences over and over again in your mind or in your conversations. A repetitive pattern, as such, does not allow the individual to move beyond that emotional experience … in essence, *it keeps us stuck!* The goal for emotional healthiness is to experience our emotions and align our emotions accurately to the present-day experience.

Let me caution you, because depending on the severity of your past hurts, you may require the assistance of psychotherapy or counseling for this step. Personally, I have attended counseling at least four times in my adult life and I am a licensed professional counselor. But it is extremely necessary that you come to this reflective view of your life when you feel safe enough to address these experiences and emotions.

Default programming is the natural conversation that you have with yourself as you process through life which drives your thinking and behaviors.

Reconnect with Your Emotions

In my experience, life circumstances forced me to reflect backward in my life, even though my body and internal script continued to fight against this reflective review. I call this resistance "my default programming or behavior." Default programming is the natural conversation that you have with yourself as you process through life which drives your thinking and behaviors. It is typically our back-up reasoning that we go to when transformation or stress seems too challenging for us.

External forces, such as a painful situation with my daughter and a lack of family support, pushed me into facing parts of my life I had been unwilling to confront for many years. Essentially, if you are able to identify the traumatic events or experiences in your past, there are benefits to participating in the exercise of examining the coping behaviors you employed to manage through your past.

Reconnecting with your emotions is a powerful resource to move forward in your life. Being able to reconnect with my emotions was centrally important for me because after the first significant trauma in my life, I stopped allowing myself to engage with my feelings in order to cope and survive.

Have you ever noticed this your life? There is a stressful situation and you think you handled the situation fine because there was no emotional outburst like crying or yelling. All seems to be going well, but some random act like someone forgetting to return your phone call, or you get cut off in traffic which causes you to blow your lid! Or when you have received great news about a job promotion and the first thing you want to do is call your closest friends and share the news; however, they are not available, and your response is to get extremely angry lashing out to your friend! The other person involved cannot understand what happened and why you reacted in that manner. These actions occurred based on how we emotionally cope with shifts or changes in our lives, whether the changes are big or small.

The Semel Institute for Neuroscience and Human Behavior (2018) classified "coping as a response to psychological stress, usually triggered by changes, in which an effort is made to maintain mental health and emotional well-being." [15] The process of managing one's mental health and emotional well-being can be activated by a pleasant or unpleasant experience in life. [15] Additional studies from the Semel Institute for Neuroscience and Human Behavior Nathanson Family Resilience Center (2018) described an unspoken component for navigating through life, as "'psychological resilience,' our ability to cope through life's inevitable adversity." [15]

The evidence-based data defined coping in different frameworks, which include "problem-solving methods," which are assertive behaviors to diminish pressure connected to life situations, or "emotional-solving methods," which are assertive activities to moderate feelings from a tense or pressure-filled situation or situations that could be tense. [5] As well, coping behaviors have been classified as, "active and avoidant" descriptors. [5] "Active coping" includes the ability to identify the stressful event and employ strategies to remediate it. [5] "Avoidance coping" includes the refusal to address the situation, causing behaviors that repudiate the issue. [5]

In my life, based on my early life experiences, I was proudly an avoidant coping individual. The word proud is used to illustrate that these avoidant coping behaviors were there for my survival. Behaviors such as

Defensiveness –
- ~ Unwilling to listen because my internal filter criticized me in a way that was unbearable to face.

- A rebuttal for any comment because I would not allow my ego to accept being wrong.
- Excuse making because it was always someone else's fault, not my own.
- Blaming or finding fault in the other person –
- Withholding any acknowledgment of my responsibility in a situation, which shifted the blame to the other person and the other person's feelings/experience un-validated.
- <u>*Creating chaotic moments to release anxiety*</u> because I did not know how to employ active coping behaviors for healthiness.

The truth is, for many years this shamefully brought me pleasure because I was releasing my repressed emotions at the cost of someone else. It grieves me to admit the truth, but it is healthier to be honest and have integrity with your own emotions. Operating in avoidant coping skills and creating chaos granted me permission to release my emotions in the most destructive patterns. This emotional cycle became the fix that I cultivated for my inability to manage my emotions.

Retreating or isolation –

- Walking away because I wanted to avoid my feelings.
- Tuning out the other person's comments to avoid my body's reaction and the tension of the situation.
- Sleeping.
- Not sharing my true thoughts or feelings, which allowed the suppression of my voice to articulate what I really felt or to share my intentions.

Coming Out!

Lashing out in anger –

- ~ Verbally abusive behaviors such as sarcasm, harsh and uncompassionate comments, or brazen responses because I learned to be passive aggressive versus articulate my truth or it felt safer using this method to deal with a situation.

Avoiding any emotions –

- ~ Pouring myself into an alternate activity, like focusing on the TV when someone is saying something that bothered me.
- ~ Fidgeting with something in my hands to distract my thoughts/emotions.
- ~ Starting a new project to keep me busy and avoiding a situation that created tension.

Controlling everything in my life –

- ~ Overly organized and rigid so I would not feel any emotions.
- ~ Imposing my influence heavily in others' lives to maintain my emotional position.
- ~ Creating an internal emotional prison for myself and an external prison-like atmosphere for those living within close proximity to me.

Reconnection to your emotions can allow you to identify the emotional coping

Reconnection to your emotions can allow you to identify the emotional coping patterns that you demonstrate in your daily life.

patterns that you are demonstrating in your daily life. I outlined my top six avoidant coping behaviors in times of stress. Also, I am now fully able to acknowledge that for many years these coping behaviors seemed effective to me. In the reconnection process, the ability to outline your emotional coping patterns will be essential to forward movement, spiritually and emotionally. It is okay to understand why you have been responding in the manner that you are choosing today. Coming from such traumatic experiences, the chosen and learned coping behaviors were my means of survival. However, these coping behaviors have caused pain/destruction in my relationships. At some point, I had to look at my chosen and learned coping behaviors and acknowledge and accept that they were no longer working. Further, I had to admit that my decision to maintain avoidant coping patterns after I became self-aware only allowed for me to be self-focused and fixated against moving forward in my life.

My coping behaviors were a part of me, and they were my vice in many ways because it was the only way I knew to deal with my emotions and stress. It did not matter if I was diminishing or someone I loved or cared about was diminished by these habits.

At some point, when going through this *Coming Out* process, you have to CARE about the impact of your coping behaviors on those in your life circle (home, work, and leisure).

Release the Impact of the Experiences

As you identify those traumatic experiences from the past, you may find linkages to where your coping behaviors emerged. Additionally, if you were never taught active coping behaviors verses avoidant coping behaviors, you will have to designate a clear plan for yourself to learn and implement active coping behaviors and replace the coping behaviors that don't serve this station in your life.

Coming Out!

After you can successfully identify your coping behaviors, the focus can shift to releasing the physical and mental impact that your emotions have in your life.

Steps to identify your coping behaviors and releasing the impact:
- ~ Retrospective analysis of the behaviors that emerged from your trauma by listing your behaviors and the thinking connected to those behaviors.
- ~ Ask trusted persons for their observations of you when in crisis or stressful moments. Write down their observations and compare to your personal list.
- ~ Be open and ready to hear information about yourself from a constructive point of view. Grant yourself permission to extend mercy to yourself as you would extend to a friend in need.
- ~ Recognize that you are the friend in need and that you are only human and ever evolving as an individual.
- ~ Look for similarities and differences in the information that you will received from the trusted and caring friend or information that you will observe about yourself.
- ~ Complete a thirty-day record of your reactions, inclusive of your thoughts and behaviors when stressed. Notate your personal observations of yourself.
- ~ List the top five behaviors and truths about your emotional health.

At the conclusion of this personal inventory of your coping reactions or responses, categorize your behaviors and thinking into two buckets – active or avoidant emotional coping patterns.

You can select the appropriate category for yourself based off of the observation exercise.

Once you have been able to identify your coping behaviors, it will be important to develop a clear plan to learn the practice of releasing your emotions in a healthy and functional way. In particularly, the emotions that have manifested physically and mentally in your life such as stress, tension, headaches, or even anxiety.

Simultaneously, take the new awareness and knowledge about yourself and look for and learn your triggers by any means necessary.

As emotions arise from your self-awareness, do not apologize for the tears, laughter, grief, glee, or healthy anger that emerges from this exercise. These emotions are a part of you and the priority is to use your strength to actively address your emotions versus to repress your emotions.

When you sense tension in your body, do not fight the emotion and do not look for an escape to expel your emotions in an unhealthy way. However, here is where teaching yourself healthier ways to express your emotions lend to you releasing your emotions in functional ways. Exercises such as:

- ~ Communication, learning to speak about your feelings is an effective activity to release the emotions you experience.
- ~ Journaling, learning to write your thoughts about your feelings provides a space for expression of your emotions. Equally, the exercise of journaling allows you to start naming your emotions.
- ~ Mindfulness Meditation, this is a mental training practice that allows you to bring yourself and your thoughts into the present, focusing on emotions, thoughts and sensations that you are physically experiencing in the here and now [18].

~ Prayer, this can be a resource for peace, relaxation, and power during this process.
~ Counseling or psychotherapy may be a helpful venue to address healthy ways to reconnect and release your emotions during and/or after the Retrospective and Reflective Analysis
~ Support group, consideration of joining a support group could be another forum for allowance of releasing the impact of your past experiences and emotions related to those experiences.

I will interject that this is a scary moment for those of us who have been avoiding emotions for many years. Learning to deal with the feelings behind the avoidant behaviors is no easy feat but it can be done!

Recognize the Power that You Possess

Recognize the power you possess to relinquish your former identity as a victim by sharing your truth, expelling the negative energies outward from your spirit, and shifting your internal script with truthful mental reframes is possible. It begins with acknowledging two important factors about yourself:

The behaviors that YOU utilized to survive your past indicates that YOU have the power and ability to shift them to NEW behaviors to live and thrive in your station of life today! Each day, thank yourself for your survival!

The resilience that YOU have and created, means that YOU have the fortitude to withstand FEELING YOUR emotions from yesterday and today! Each day, remind yourself that you are safe now to live and thrive!

Dealing with the feelings behind my avoidant coping behaviors was necessary to move forward! It is a significant truth revealed to me in my *Coming Out* process! Truthfully, each day of my current life, I am allowing myself to experience these emotions because I have over thirty to forty years of avoided emotions to process and release in a healthy way. Oftentimes, well-meaning people in my life have made comments such as, "Do not get upset about this or that," but the reality of this type of statement implies that I ignore what is going on in my body emotionally, mentally, and physically. It is more productive holistically for each of us to employ active coping around our emotions. In instances where others seek to help me by telling me not to get upset, I firmly explain that I am not upset, and I need to experience my emotions in a healthy way. I ask them to refrain from those comments and provide me with the space for my response to my emotions. I then move into an internal dialogue within myself. The questions that I pose to myself consist of: a) What is the real issue bothering me? b) What control do I have in this situation? c) Have I given myself permission to experience my feelings to release any tension? d) What do I need right now? and e) What is my plan forward?

Reconnecting to your emotions is a process where you provide allowance to yourself. This means that you do not want to judge the emotions, particularly if you don't know how to name the emotion. Seeking to not judge yourself for an emotion, gives you freedom to tell yourself these truths:

~ You are safe.
~ You can feel.
~ Your emotions are natural.

~ You are bringing yourself into healthiness.
~ Your feelings are not wrong.

When seeking to change your internal and external language about your emotions, it is important for you to give yourself permission to see the healthy or functional side of emotions. For example, this would look like not describing every emotion you feel as an expression of anger. Additionally, this would mean building your language around emotions where there was a previous negative frame, such as we had an argument over a matter. The positive reframe would be that we participated in a vibrant discussion on a matter where you and the other party articulated passionate points of views. Perhaps, you speak and express the emotions in terms that you are most familiar with from the lack of reconnection to your emotions and language around your emotions.

On the next page, you will find an image of the "Emotional Wheel" by Robert Plutchik as a tool to expand your emotion vocabulary. [13] This tool provides outlines of different emotions that we can express, and it can be a useful guide as you seek to recognize the power you possess to move forward in this area.

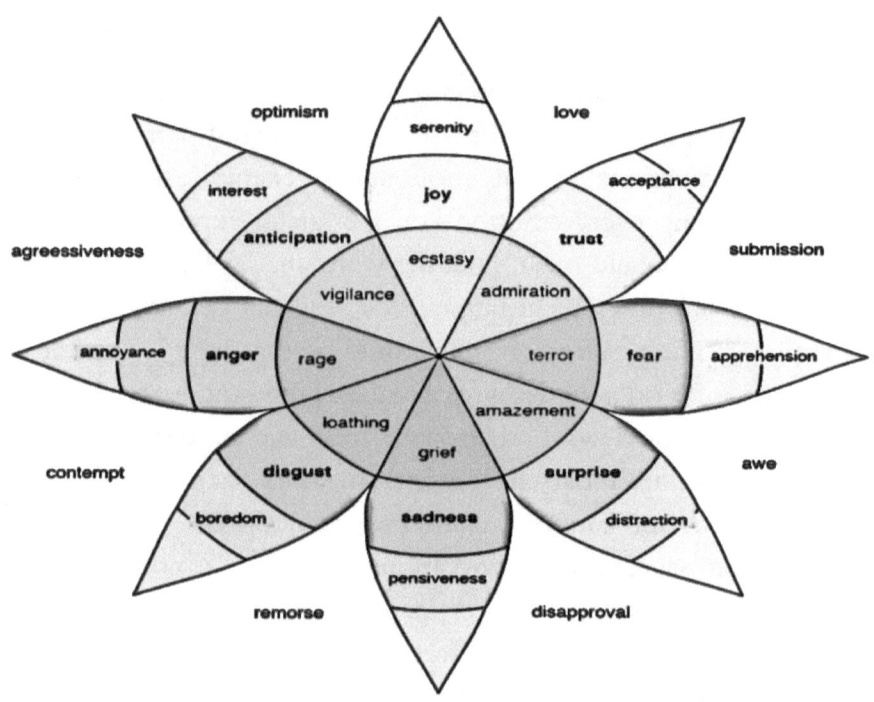

"The Emotional Wheel" by Robert Plutchik [13]

4

Fighting for You is Paramount!

If you are a fan of the Rocky sequels, you have come to learn that the storyline is based on a fighter whose life is full of small battles, but the fighter's most significant battle is against his greatest foe. His foe is a bigger and better fighter. He has to retrain his heart, mind, body, and soul to defeat his larger than life opponent. It is an infamous scene in the Rocky sequels where the song, "Gonna Fly Now" plays like an anthem and Rocky determines in order to win the fight of his life, he must fight for himself! His trainer cannot win the fight, nor can his fame, it is his resolve, his focus, and his intention that must shift to beat his monstrous opponent! [20] We see this play out through a two-hour movie and into the final boxing match scene, where Rocky ends up as the victor.

Being a child sexual abuse survivor and now a life thriver, I held a childhood, cartoonish, and almost heroic fantasy that someone would come and save me. This dream or fantasy developed early on my life, when I was being sexually abused. I silently carried this hope and fantasy throughout my teen and adult years. I was constantly looking for my hero, my savior, the one who would fight for me. There was a subconscious piece of my soul desiring a fairy tale man to be the person who rescued me from the men who abused me. I recall even daydreaming about this powerful and momentous time, while internally growing more and more angry because no one ever showed up to fight for me or to rescue me!

All the while, no one knew that I needed someone to fight for me and to rescue me, as I continued to present myself to the world as a strong, accomplished, and put together individual. However, the converse took place in my life, I became the fighter! However, I was not fighting for me to live, but only to survive in abuse mentality! I fought to be the perpetual victim. I fought to be misunderstood. I fought to deprive myself of love and acceptance. I fought to ignore my needs and my pain. I fought to stay stuck in unhealthiness. The fight was internal and external as I found a reason to argue, be combative, and brazen with others because it felt good to my damaged soul.

I was not fighting for my soul to be free, for my peace, for my self-love or my progress. Until one day in a conversation when I was crying and sharing my frustrations with life, exclaiming that the pain was too excruciating and the challenges with motherhood were more than I could bare because I could not stop the internal and external abuse cycle in my life. The other individual disagreed and told me that I spend all of my energy fighting those who care for me and those who don't care for me. But there was a question this person posed that opened my eyes to my own power. She asked me, "Why can't you use the same energy you use to fight everyone and fight for yourself?"

This question left me perplexed, so I decided to pray. I contemplated until my truth met my unspoken and un-tapped power to fight for me! In a miraculous

> No one knew that I needed someone to fight for me and to rescue me!

and enlightening moment, I realized the only way to truly COME OUT was for Lisa to FIGHT FOR Lisa! I was the person that I was looking for!! God had given me ... ME!

With that experience, I made a decision within myself to turn my energy for me, instead of against me.

One of the biggest fights you may have is with your inner child, who may still rule or wants to rule you. My inner child always won over my will in my life because for the majority of my life my inner child felt unsafe. My inability to discipline my inner child caused me to feel justified in hurting others, especially those I loved. In the process of fighting for Lisa, it was time for me to tell the young girl Lisa that she could let go because I was ready to fight for her, with my whole self. From there, I committed my whole self to discovering healthier ways to operate in my life. I communicated to the little girl Lisa, the teenage Lisa, and the adult woman Lisa that I was moving in courage, not by losing her but loving her, forgiving her, and growing into maturity. This was a critical step in the process because the inner child needs to align to your adult self.

*Please note that inner child work may require the assist of a therapeutic environment. It will be important that you use self-awareness and seek out clinical assistance, if needed.

Inner child work can be a powerful tool to come out of the patterns in your life that you seek to change or resolve. Dr. Stephen Diamond contended in his forthcoming

> I realized the only way to truly COME OUT was for Lisa to FIGHT FOR Lisa! I was the person that I was looking for!! God had given me ... ME!

book, *"Psychotherapy for the Soul: Thirty-Three Essential Secrets for Emotional and Spiritual Self-Healing."*, that many adults today have not addressed the reality of their inner child. [4] Additionally, that acknowledgement of the inner child would benefit many adults in navigating their person and their life. [4] Further, a recent study, *The Efficacy of an Intervention on Healing the Inner Child On Emotional Intelligence, and Adjustment Among the College Students"*, conducted on college age learners to address inner child healing produced affirmative results on emotional intelligence and adjustment levels. [16]

I became conscious to the fact that my inner child was destroying my relationships and stifling my growth because my inner child was ruling me as an adult. My fear began with her, my need to control began with her being abused, and my esteem was stunted as a child. I needed to commence the work of telling my inner child that I love her and I forgive her for not telling anyone about the abuse and that I accept her completely. I needed to esteem her for her value as a human and honor her as someone whom came to this earth with purpose and promise! It was important to share with my inner child that I am growing up to be a mature adult woman and that she can't have the space in my adult life anymore.

"An understanding and conversation with your inner child may look like this..."

I thanked her for being there for me and teaching me skills that were useful, but I also acknowledged to her that it is time to relinquish many of those skills as my life is different today. I confirmed with her that I am safe, and I am accepting self-love, as well as healthy love from others. Also, I informed her that I'm valuing myself and my daughter and my inner child can no longer be jealous of my love for my daughter because when I love and value my daughter, I love and value her!

Coming Out!

How Does Fighting for Yourself Apply to Your Life?

A recognition that you have more strength in you than you can possibly imagine could be unbelievable and scary. The issue is that you have not tapped into your power yet, nor have you fully grasped and accepted your power!

Furthermore, fighting for you is an all-day and everyday intentional commitment to yourself! There is daily work for growth that can include meditation to address your inner child. Secure your inner child and tell your inner child, he/she is okay to let you grow up from the emotional arrest and the coping that helped you survive the past trauma, mistreatment, or disappointment. This is crucial!

Remember that changing your language matters as you fight for yourself. Analyze the words you use which are limiting or holding back your progress. For instance, I used to say, "I'm *trying to* do or I'm *going to* learn," but the use of each of those passive verbs were coaxing my spirit not to change or to be accountable for change. Internal self-communication should have the language of progress and of power!

Understand that God has given us free will and each day we have the power to create the life we want. If you desire a life where you believe people will hurt you and no one understands you, then you will create that life for yourself. However, if you want to take your power and create a life where anger, resentment, and blame do not dictate your thinking and actions, you have that power as well. You may have been abused but you do not have to choose to abuse others or create a life where you still get abused, this also includes whether you are choosing to abuse yourself, your mind, or your body.

It's really truly up to you! Give your power to no one and stop thinking you have power over anyone but YOU! Believe in you and you can usher in peace, love, and joy in your life and it will manifest itself!

Staying stuck in past trauma will only slowly destroy you, mentally, emotionally and physically, which produces a life where you will never let yourself truly live!

We don't get any do overs in this life!!! It is truly your mind over matter! Choose a different way because you are your Best Advocate! You are a Fighter. You are a WARRIOR! Warrior implies there is a victory, and as Rocky was determined to beat his biggest foe, so can you!

Personal Coming Out Journey Work
Reconnecting with Your Emotions ~ Awareness

It is important to revisit the pain associated to your past experiences because it helps you unlock those experiences so you can:

~ Reconnect with your emotions in order to feel again.
~ Do you have any apprehensions about experiencing your feelings?
~ Can you sense a longing within to allow yourself the freedom to emote?

Release the impact these experiences may have had on your physical body and your mental self, inclusive of being present with those emotions.

~ Have you noticed any physical issues due to your emotion management styles?
~ What would you experience if you could be present with your emotions?

Recognize the power you possess to relinquish your former identity as a victim by sharing your truth, expelling the negative energies outward from your spirit, and shifting your internal script with truthful mental reframes.

~ Are you afraid to tap into your personal power?
~ Can you see yourself making these power personal shifts?

Steps to identify your coping behaviors and releasing the impact:

- Retrospectively analyze the behaviors that emerged from your trauma by listing your behaviors and thinking that is connected to those behaviors.
- Ask trusted persons for their observations of you when in crisis or stressful moments. Write down their observations and compare to your personal list.
- Be open and ready to hear information about yourself from a constructive point of view.
- Grant yourself permission to extend mercy to yourself as you would extend to a friend in need.
- Recognize that you are the friend in need and that you are only human and ever evolving as an individual.
- Look for similarities and differences in the information you received from the trusted and caring friend or information that you observe about yourself.
- Complete a thirty-day record of your reactions, inclusive of your thoughts and behaviors when stressed. Notate your personal observations of yourself.
- List the top five behaviors and truths about your emotional health.

At the conclusion of this personal inventory of your coping reactions or responses, categorize your behaviors and thinking into two brackets – active or avoidant emotional coping patterns.

You can select the appropriate category for yourself based off the observation exercise.

How would you classify your coping methods? Why did you make that decision?

"Active coping" includes the ability to identify the stressful event and employ strategies to remediate it. [2]

"Avoidance coping" includes the refusal to address the situation, causing behaviors that repudiate the issue. [2]

How can I work to change my language around once I am able to reconnect to my emotions?

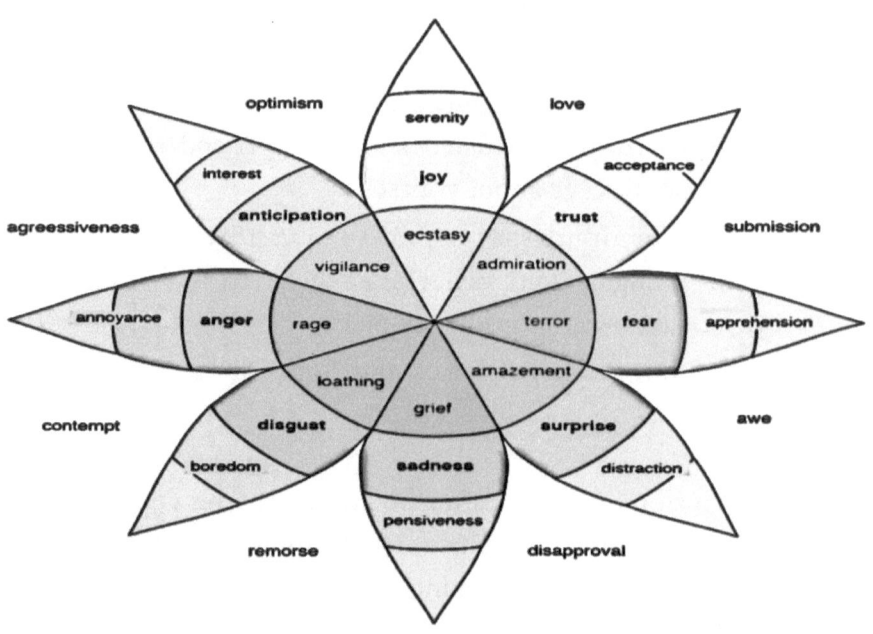

"The Emotional Wheel" by Robert Plutchik [13]

Coming Out!

- ✓ Choose an emotion from the chart that you are not familiar with expressing.
- ✓ Look up the meaning of the emotion.
- ✓ Look up a pictorial or description of this emotion.
- ✓ Ask yourself if this is an emotion that you can choose to feel that expresses what you are actually feeling?
- ✓ Try it and try talking about your feelings.
- ✓ Make a conscious effort to speak about how you are displaying this emotion.
- ✓ Try this exercise for twenty-one-days for consistency and practice.
- ✓ Journal and share your experience to gain further insight about yourself.

Recap Steps to Assist You Fighting for You:

- ~ Recognize that God gave you to fight for You!
- ~ Open your eyes to witness the love that encompasses your life.
- ~ Surround yourself with love. Start with practicing self-love.
- ~ Secure support from those whom truly love and believe in you.
- ~ Tap into your personal power.
- ~ Consider inner child work (therapeutically guided, if needed).
- ~ Identify your negative or unhealthy trends in language because it is a result of your unspoken internal messages.
- ~ Continue the daily work of reflective and retrospective analysis as needed.
- ~ Continue the work to unpack your traumatic events and their meaning now and then.

- Reconnect with your emotions and become present with them.
- Take the twenty-one-day new emotion expression challenge.
- Find an accountability person.
- Get to it.

Section 3
Recognition of the Power of Your Voice and Your Strength
~ Acknowledgement

5

Coming Out Commences ~ Acknowledgment and Acceptance Principle

Self-awareness encompasses the *Coming Out* process. You will move from self-awareness to an honest acknowledgment of your self-discoveries and from there you go forward to personal acceptance. This progression equates to your acceptance of all the choices that you willfully made in your life. This includes those choices you completed where you do not understand the full reason for those decisions. There was an unspoken need that your choices sought to fill in your life. The *Coming Out* experience gives allowance for self-acceptance and self-love to bridge peace and happiness within oneself. Additionally, the *Coming Out* experience initiates the breakdown of guilt, shame, and secrets that may have prevented growth, freedom, and peace.

> **The bottom line is ... if you cannot tell yourself the truth, you will never tell the next person the truth!**

Coming Out!

Acknowledgement and Acceptance Principle

The process of acknowledgment and acceptance is a personal, internal empowerment and transformation that can yield external physiological and emotional results. I developed this principle as I travailed through my *Coming Out* experience.

The premise for Acknowledgement and Acceptance Principle operates under sincere authenticity; however, there is a bottom line. The bottom line is … if you cannot tell yourself the truth, you will never tell the next person the truth! Telling yourself the truth is not always an easy process, but it is necessary for forward movement!

Each individual may carry part of their life history that is challenging for them. Your history could be too painful and the memories have been pushed deep into the recesses of your mind. There could be an embarrassing situation and you possess a fear of judgment, and addressing the embarrassing situation could impact your self-image. It could be that you carry a false sense of self, which suggests that if you tell yourself the truth, you could face rejection of yourself. It could be an issue of pride where seeing your truth makes you conclude that you are less than. Or it could be an area where you are an overly critical person, where seeing the truth about yourself can cause a false sense of judgment.

There are many different areas, as we are all different people with differing experiences, that could conflict with the acknowledgment and acceptance process. Nevertheless, the acknowledgment and acceptance process will be the same for each of us.

My discovery of the Four-A's Principle came from my interaction with the serenity prayer associated with the twelve-step recovery movement. It may seem like a meaningless recitation of words, but it is not! It was the catalyst that fostered my thinking on the value of the acknowledgement and acceptance process, within the Four-A's Principle.

The key that I found regarding the serenity prayer...is you cannot only recite the prayer, but it is necessary to break the prayer down for your own personal application. The serenity prayer reads:

"God grant me the serenity to accept the things that I cannot change, the courage to change the things that I can and wisdom to know the difference." [1]

Let's examine four of the words in this prayer:
Serenity = the state of being calm, peaceful, and untroubled
Acceptance = the action of consenting to receive or undertake something offered
Courage = the ability to do something that frightens one
Wisdom = the quality of having experience, knowledge, and good judgment

After the recitation of the prayer, the question you can ask yourself is, "How bad do I really want to be in a state of being calm, peaceful, and untroubled?"

If you apply the prayer for personal application and you can read it as follows:

"I am asking God (Higher Power) for a calm, peaceful, and an untroubled disposition in my spirit. I am recognizing that entangled in God granting my request is my ability, my choice, my power, and my will to let go and/or consent to what is available to me.

What is Available to You?

Coming Out!

The offer is peace, power, choice, and transformation. The simple act of your will to *believe* in someone greater or God, opens up your ability to release and to receive.

What are You Releasing?

You release doubt and choose faith in God, along with belief in yourself! In this transactional act of choice and power, you are transforming spiritually to receive a calm, peace, and an untroubled disposition. Additionally, your choice fosters your ability to move forward, not necessarily without fear, *but with a choice to tell yourself the truth no matter what the truth reveals.* In the moment of <u>acknowledgment of your truth</u>, you receive the gift of honor and power. Personal honor and power actualization propels the experience of inner achievement within your spirit.

Now, there is a desire to take another step forward. The ability to move forward to healthiness, despite any lingering anxiousness or fears, indicates the honor and power that you have granted yourself. God is moving to grant you with the ability to do something that may frighten you, which is to <u>accept the truth</u>, despite what the truth is, so you can gain wisdom and self-acceptance. Despite any anxiousness, negativity, or any other emotions sparked by acceptance of your truth, you can feel safe enough to look at past experiences and gain knowledge (wisdom) of what has not worked and what has worked. Then you can make a choice to trust yourself to move forward and at the same time trust in God. In this moment, <u>acceptance</u> can offer you a new route or a new choice in the area that you are facing, which is the goal.

You may have been saying to yourself and others that I just want peace, but do you really? The peace you are seeking requires the acknowledgment of the truth, not just your truth, but solely the truth that matches with empirical evidence in your life.

Acknowledgment Begins with…

Acknowledge the totality of who you are, your history, your thoughts, your drive, and yourself in the present day.

Acknowledge that you can exist with a state of being calm, peaceful, and untroubled.

Acknowledgement means you tell the truth about what is right in front of you.

Acknowledge the fantasies that may have captured your mind about yourself.

Acknowledge the strengths and abilities that are true about yourself.

Acknowledge that you are worthy of love, honor, choice, value, self-care, protection, and growth.

Acknowledge any faulty thinking that could be hindering your growth.

Acknowledgement means you tell the truth about what is right in front of you.

Coming Out!

Acknowledgment Chart- This chart allows you to see the truth in your life based on empirical evidence. See an example below of how I completed the Acknowledgment Chart.

ACKNOWLEDGEMENT CHART (based on empirical evidence) **Who are you?**	Empirical evidence that supports this truth – what is the evidence/why does the evidence support this truth?	What you tell yourself.	What is true?
A person who is worthy of love.	Daily blessings such as life, my body functioning appropriately, people in my life extending love in a variety of ways – phone calls, birthday texts, spending time with me.	No one cares or really loves me.	I am worthy of love.
A person who argues a lot.	At home, I dispute almost everything that my daughter says. At work, I get angry way too easily. Why? – pent up anger that is not fully released, self-criticism, and projection of insecurities to my daughter or others.	It is my default thinking to believe others are attacking me or to be defensive.	I am still angry with life because there is no forgiveness in my heart for myself.

Acceptance Begins with…

Accepting that the path forward is not without fear, but that you can move forward with fear that contains a courageous energy.

Accepting that you possess the courage to really see yourself as you are and your potential to grow.

Accepting that the truth in front of you … is what it is; do not rationalize the truth into something else.

Accepting your present and existing power to evaluate the truth, and why it is true based on your experiences and/or empirical evidence.

Accepting that you can actualize good judgment and make a different choice based on what you know about yourself today.

Accepting that you can live in your truth and it will not break you and that your acceptance of truth will only strengthen you.

Accepting that you may have harmed yourself or others, and if you are able to … seek to make an amends (only if making amends is not harmful for you or the other person).

Accepting that the path forward is not without fear, but that you can move forward with fear that contains a courageous energy.

Coming Out!

Acknowledgement and Acceptance Chart - This chart allows you to see the truth in your life based on empirical evidence and use your power of acceptance. See an example below of how I completed the Acknowledgment and Acceptance Chart.

ACKNOWLEDGMENT and ACCEPTANCE CHART
(based on empirical evidence)

Who are you?	Empirical evidence that supports this truth – what is the evidence/why does the evidence support this truth?	What you tell yourself.	What is true?	Can I accept this truth about myself? (yes/no)	What choices do I have or can I make now with this truth?
A person worthy of love.	Daily blessings such as life, my body functioning appropriately, people in my life extending love in a variety of ways – phone calls, birthday texts, spending time with me.	No one cares or really loves me.	I am worthy of love.	YES	I can tell myself each day that every essence of me is worthy of love. I accept when healthy/good love comes to me and send gratitude to God/universe.
A person who argues a lot.	At home, I dispute almost everything that my daughter says. At work, I get angry way too easily.	It is my default thinking to believe others are attacking me or to be defensive.	I am still angry with life because there is no forgiveness in my heart for me.	YES	I can become more aware when I am acting out of this unhealthy characteristic and course-correct or acknowledge my behavior – no self-punishment, just self-correction.

6

Coming Out Shame and Victim Mentality

Oftentimes, as women, we carry an outward demeanor of strength, but inwardly we are delicate as a flower. Sometimes in our lives there is shame that no one is aware of and this shame is like a hidden decay that can wilt the petals of a person's soul.

This can be a delicate topic for many of the individuals who have been abused or who currently are in abuse situations. Why? It is because the entire stance of abuse carries the umbrella of shame.

> Today, I accept God's purpose in my existence, and I remind myself daily that there is nothing wrong with me.

For so long I have lived as the scared little girl, then as the young woman who tried to change herself dramatically so that my past could not catch up with me or frame me negatively. As a result of the abuse I endured throughout my childhood, I was full of self-hatred and disapproval of myself.

Coming Out!

Today, I accept God's purpose in my existence, and I remind myself daily that there is nothing wrong with me. However, for many years, I suffered in silence about my abuse and lived under the pressure of my abuser's presence.

As with many young girls and boys, my abusers were males in my family, my sister's husband, and her husband's twin brother. My abuse happened early in life and continued until my high school years. I share this part of my history to expose it and to release it from the grip of shame and judgment. I do not share it for sympathy, but I share it so that I can provide empathy of my own experiences and continue my fight to healthiness.

It is understandable that each person who has experienced sexual abuse trauma, from molestation to rape, has a right to never disclose this truth to anyone. IT IS THEIR RIGHT and THEIR CHOICE of disclosure or non-disclosure! We live in a society in which one in nine girls and one in fifty-three boys will experience sexual abuse before eighteen years of age. [2] Additionally, mental health issues are found in many adults who have experienced this childhood trauma. [2] However, it is each individual's prerogative to share or not share their experiences. For my *Coming Out* process, it was vitally important that I bring this truth to the light of day and move forward for my own mental health.

The Muzzle Removed

I was working at a residential adolescent home with young people who were wards of the State of Illinois as a Quality Improvement Coordinator. At that time, I shared an office with two other ladies in my department. One random day, my co-worker began to share about her past sexual abuse by her father and I found myself encouraging and comforting her. Her willingness to share her experience, started to spark my contemplation regarding talking about my past abuse. I eventually shared a portion of my story with my co-worker as our relationship developed a higher level of trust. Prior to my sharing, I recall feeling as if I had a muzzled on my mouth that would not allow me to speak about my abuse. Psychologically, I could not even manage the words audibly, so when I decided to share a portion of my abuse history, it was a huge deal for me!

After opening up a little bit to my co-worker, who is now my dear friend, I started to pursue counseling to further explore my past abuse and its impact on my life. That was seventeen years ago when I first sought out counseling for my sex abuse trauma. As I gained more power within my voice to share my past abuse, I eventually shared with two family members. It turned out to be an unsupportive experience for me, which caused me to not share it again to my family for fifteen years.

One of the first things that you must decide within yourself is: Are you ready to share what happen to you? When you make this decision, please find someone you can trust to support you through the sharing process.

Over the years, I have continued to utilize mental health services periodically, such as counseling and support groups, as I find them to be a great resource for myself.

I encourage each person who has experienced any form of trauma to seek out mental health services. Research the counselor, as it is important to find the right fit and counseling style for you. Counselors and/or therapists practice with different theoretical and therapeutic frameworks, so conducting sound research is wise.

If counseling is not the place that you disclose, it helps to find a trusted friend who can support you. I found that my family was not a place of trust or support to disclose my past abuse. Even though they were not supportive, I eventually shared my abuse with more of my family a few years ago; however, at that point, I shared for the purpose of my healing versus seeking their support. My goal was to release the shame and bring exposure to my experience.

However, throughout the years, I began to have experiences where sharing my abuse was helpful to other women and young girls when telling their abuse experiences. As I taught in Christian conferences and retreats, I saw the life impact of *Coming Out* of my shame to tell my sexual abuse history.

I would argue that when you are able, discover how your abuse history can be transitional to someone else's life, and you will see that the muzzle that silenced you can start to shift open. The shame that captured your tongue starts to unleash because you appreciate that there is commonality and power in talking about your experiences with others who have similar stories but have never spoken on it.

Protection of Shame

> **Coming Out of shame is more than just telling others about your experience, it is understanding what you were seeking to protect with that shame.**

Coming Out of shame is more than just telling others about your experience, it is understanding what you were seeking to protect with that shame.

I wanted to protect my image of me within myself. I believed deep down there was something amiss in me for me to be the victim of abuse. Shame kept me holding on to the damaged view of myself. I had become accustomed to this perspective.

I wanted to protect my family, even though they did not protect me. To be fair, they did not know about the abuse; however, my sister was aware and never spoke to me about it until years later. But I wanted to protect the family's image. I wanted to keep my relationship intact with my family since I had lost them when I was younger. Shame kept me sacrificing my own well-being for the sake of protecting the emotions and un-comfortability of my family. I knew it would put them in challenging situations where I would want them to choose me over the other sibling. I also knew deep down that they would never do that for me.

Shame causes you to punish yourself for a crime that you did not commit!

Shame is like a dark cloud because it imposes lies to your soul and psyche.

Shame is dirty and leaves you with a stench of the abuser's manipulation in your thoughts and dreams.

Shame pushes you into hiding; thus, you hold on to it for life.

Shame causes you to blame yourself and ask yourself, why you?

Shame causes you to stay stuck in a state of self-criticism.

Shame is like sitting in a room clouded with smoke from cigarettes.

As the smoke swirls around and the visibility becomes poor, you are only visible in the places where the smoke has not taken over. You are there and you are noticeable, but you are not seen in your fullest capacity. The shame that sexual abuse carries causes you to stay in the smoked-filled room, hidden by the pockets of smoke, when the door to leave the room and get fresh air is right before you.

Coming Out of the shame is a process similar to standing up in the smoke-filled room, walking to the door, opening the door, and walking out. For me, *Coming Out* of shame allowed me to clear the air, release the darkness, and put the onus back on the perpetrators of my abuse. I no longer wanted or needed to carry their evil deeds on me. Talking about my abuse allowed the lingering stench of shame to slowly dissipate. Focusing on renewing my thinking daily while fostering a new perspective became a vital daily activity!

Steps to Come Out of shame:
- ~ Acknowledge the truth – the abuse did happen.
- ~ Accept the loss that you experienced.
- ~ Accept that you are not in prison or captive to the abuser anymore.
- ~ Accept that no matter the circumstances of your abuse experience, you were not responsible. *This may take a lot of clinical work to allow yourself to stop taking responsibility for your abuse.
- ~ Expose the abuse in some form or fashion, despite the length of time since the abuse occurred.
- ~ Remove the muzzle from your mouth and speak it out so you can experience telling the truth.
- ~ Forgive yourself for not telling anyone.
- ~ Practice living in the light within by instituting honesty and integrity.

One of my biggest hurdles was finding a way to stop keeping secrets. Shame promotes secrecy and I became a professional at the pathology of keeping secrets. I often chose not to disclose even when there was not a shameful circumstance or situation to hold or protect. It takes diligence and intentional practice to illuminate truth and to foster new ways of operating outside of shame.

Coming Out of Victim Mentality

A *victim* is defined in the Oxford Online Dictionary (2018) as: a) A person harmed, injured, or killed as a result of a crime, accident, or other event or action; b) A person who is tricked or duped; c) A person who has come to feel helpless and passive in the face of misfortune or ill-treatment; and d) A living creature killed as a religious sacrifice. [14] For the purposes of this discussion, definitions a, b and c could apply for my life.

I would like to begin with this real, poignant truth: "No one asks to be a victim under any circumstance!" Additionally, "No one wears a sign or puts their name on a billboard, so all in the universe can read that this individual is asking to be made a victim!" This is simply not the case, whether you come from a religious background and believe that sin within our world created the climate for the creation of victims, or you believe life just happens where some are fortunate to not experience victimization, or you believe that some will experience victimization over the course of their life. Either way, in the world we live in, people are subject to a victim experience.

> **Being a victim was my unspoken crutch. I was completely unaware of how this mentality oozed out of every part of me.**

Some of these victim experiences are unexplainable, horrible, and so devastating that one may want to forget them all together or completely erase their mind from revisiting them. If this applies to you and you are reading this book, you may need to walk through this journey with the assistance of a therapist, counselor, or life coach.

However, I am sharing my victim mentality and my process of *Coming Out* with the hopes that it can be a guide or catalyst to your freedom in this area.

It one-hundred percent pains me to admit that being a victim was my unspoken crutch. I was completely unaware of how this mentality oozed out of every part of me. Victim mentality created an injurious space for me because I resisted letting this part of me go ... this was my drug. My victim mentality fed me; as I previously explained to you, I felt emotionally unsupported in so many ways and being a victim allowed me to get support.

Perversion crept into my victim mentality as I would sometimes imagine getting severely injured in the hopes that people rallied to my side with concern. The movie in my mind always ended with me being cared for after such a tragic event took place in my life. However, this was not my reality at all.

In every situation, I needed people to feel sorry for me so I could get my needs met. It did not matter if the person was a family member, my daughter, a co-worker, a friend, a male partner, or a therapist, I tried to find a way to get my needs met by being a victim. The person that I sucked the most support and care from was my daughter. I was unaware that I poisoned our relationship with my victim mentality until she became older and began to articulate her frustrations about our relationship.

Victim mentality sometimes presents as selfishness to others, but in your mind, you have convinced yourself that you have this mentality because most people don't give you what you need, so you will use your unspoken victim status to claim it.

Victim mentality seeks out male or female relationships who look for individuals to save them. Also, the victim mentality puts a lot of pressure on those individuals to rescue them from a past that cannot be changed. All the while, you refuse to take the necessary steps to help rescue yourself at the suggestions of those people in your life.

I recall the previous relationship that I had with my daughter's father; he was often vocal about his observation of my family dynamic and things that I could do differently, so I could start to rescue myself, but I refused to hear him. Actually, I would get angry with him for even mentioning such things to me. I would often think to myself, "What gives him the right to say these things to me?" But the truth was that I gave him the right because my victim mentality set up the stage for him to try to rescue me.

Victim mentality comes out in your language. For instance, I recall myself saying things like, "I have a half-brother and half-sister on my father's side, but they don't like me." Now, the statement is true, but it was my secret motivation for the statement to set the stage for me to receive a fix for my victim status. My intentions were to play the victim, so the hearer could say something encouraging or sympathetic to me because of this reality.

Victim mentality manifested itself when I had an argument or disagreement where someone pointed out a flaw or something I did that bothered or hurt them. I would, with great precision, be able to shift the conversation to what they did to me. Never acknowledging how my actions could have caused the disagreement or what I could do differently because I only wanted the person to do something for me. My mind told me that I was the only victim in the scenario.

Coming Out!

Victim mentality opens up an unspoken pathology in your thinking and behaviors that can even allow you to re-create your sexual abuse scenario in your adult life. My victim mentality created blind spots for me, which put my daughter at risk. At times, we don't even recognize that we have a victim mentality because it has become ingrained in who we believe we are and the life we create for ourselves because of this pathology.

I was so scared of my true voice and poor in my thinking that I allowed my childhood abuser to be in my life. He was at my first wedding. He was around my child. On a family vacation, at the determent of myself, I went to my abusers' (my sister's husband and twin brother) home for the sake of my family (my sister decided that this is where we would go and take my mother while on a family vacation). My victim mentality convinced me to not speak up for my mental health or my well-being. But my victim mentality lied to me and told me that I was over what they did to me. I sat there, uncomfortably with my daughter, as an adult woman with no power, pretending I was okay in the presence of my childhood rapists. Victim mentality is powerful and dangerous all at the same time! We must become aware of our choices due to this pathology.

Coming Out of your victim mentality means you have to seek conscious awareness of your thinking as a result of your abuse. It was when a nice guy asked me out that I started to notice my thoughts were focused on how he would respond to me in a sensual or romantic way. But yet, I did not want this relationship. When I started to become aware of my victim mentality, I was reluctant to move too fast in relationships with men as I did not want it to be driven off my abuse thinking. I just wanted friendships with men verses romantic relationships.

What is abuse thinking? Honestly, it can vary for each individual, but for me, I noticed these things any time a male displayed interest: Things such as:

- ~ The guy had to chase me verses me expressing my own interest in him.
- ~ I would start seeing sensual imagery and tell myself that if we were physically intimate, then he will be hooked!
- ~ I liked being liked even if I did not like the guy.
- ~ I used sexual prow-less to get attention-flirtation, being coy with eye contact, etc.

All of these thoughts and behaviors were based off years of my abuse-thinking, where I considered my body as the only thing I had to offer a man. I had to own that this was my thinking, so I could start to change it. I started a simple but powerful true affirmation: "I am more than what my body offers!" I only saw myself as a usable object for a man, but it was my abuse-thinking. It can control you when you don't even know it. It takes willingness and effort to reverse this thinking into a healthier thought pattern. The actions I described in my abuse-thinking could be perfectly normal in a non-victim mentality mode of operation.

Each of us may have different ways the victim mentality plays out in our living space, but make no mistake, until you make a conscious and deliberate effort every day, you will stay stuck in this mentality and pathology.

Here are the truths I had to come to understand and accept:

- ~ I had to stop looking to be rescued. Why did I need to make this shift? It is because the little girl who needed to be rescued is now a safe, grown woman. That little girl and I had to accept that I was okay, and I could use my own power to rescue myself.

- ~ I had to accept that my past could not change and then grieve what I felt I'd lost so I could stop searching for it in my present and future.
- ~ I had to change my language and learn to speak with accountability for my actions and with confidence about what I needed.
- ~ I had to learn what were my actual needs, so I could determine what real actions I needed to do to get my needs met in functional ways. For instance, I learned that one of my needs is to feel supported, so I had to implement things into my life where I was getting supported verses manipulating a situation for support.

Victimhood becomes one's identity when there is no other identity that one can accept or associate themselves to. The idea that you are powerless over others can often lead to controlling behaviors like intimidation, insults, shutting others down, outbursts, or using their failures to validate your victim mentality and lifestyle. Admitting the truth about these behaviors are important acknowledgments and actions needed to release you from this mentality.

Acceptance that you had no control over the person that hurt or mistreated you is paramount! This is a true statement no matter how the situation took place or how the situation left you to perceive life thereafter. You may have believed you contributed in some way to your mistreatment, but it is simply not the truth. You never held a desire to be mistreated, traumatized, or hurt. Even if you misjudged the situation or the person, you still have to choose to practice *your ability* to <u>accept</u>

that you did not make another person act in certain behaviors. They made a choice to input their unhealthy way of living into your life space and, up to now, you accepted this lie as your own. NOW you must take your power, honor yourself, and value your truth.

Acceptance that you had no control over the person that hurt or mistreated you is paramount.

Release your need to blame or accept responsibility for their behavior! Release your need to be a person who gets off from victimhood mentality and living!

Ask yourself how your soul or mind is fed by choosing to be a victim or practicing this mentality! Write down where victim mentality serves you and write down where it impedes you. You may need to ask someone else to help you with this exercise.

What are the actions that can be implemented to *Coming Out* of a victim mentality?

Create a revelation/vision –
> Imagine what your life would look like if you did not operate from a victim mentality. Learn your default thinking and behaviors (this will help you identify when you are operating in victim mentality).
> ~ Describe this image in pictorial terms (draw or get images to get a visual view of your revelation).
> ~ Use your personal power to implement your pictorial revelation into practice.
> ~ Determine which steps you will take first in the revelation plan

- This could be a morning routine that includes meditation and affirmations.
- This could also include personal notes or quotes placed on your mirror and/or around your home.
- This could be a personal message that you record on your phone to play to yourself four times a day.
- Take action on what you decide to do for yourself.
- Incorporate support partners – a trusted friend, a life coach or a therapist/counselor.

7

Coming Out of Non-Forgiveness of Yourself and Guilt

Ponder this ... if a parent lives in guilt for the failures to meet the expectations of parentage and the child lives in regret or in a feeling of missing out, then what space does that leave between them? The space is guilt for the parent and anger for the child...

This chapter has been the toughest for me to write because I carried so much guilt for not knowing myself well enough before becoming a parent. I would argue that it is better for adults to be healthy and functional individuals as they consider introducing children to this world. Let me say, we all contend with one or two elements of dysfunction but going into parenting without any awareness of your needs or struggles can be very damaging to the children and family as a whole.

My Guilt and My Non-Forgiveness

In my case as a parent, I loved my daughter, but my skills were limited in expressing emotional love based on my learned experience and past trauma. My retrospective historical analysis revealed my truth, which included growing up in an environment where my physical needs were met but my emotional needs were not. I knew what it looked like to display love through provision, but I did not know how to encourage, or to be emotionally supportive or to just be present because I was too busy reliving my past as a mother and as an individual.

My lack of skills to nurture, to display empathy, and to be emotionally present left my child with insecurities about my care for her, not my love for her. As I was unaware of the messages that I believed and lived by, I left my daughter vulnerable and alone to navigate portions of her life where she really needed me the most. I carried immense guilt due to this fact. In 2014, I remember lying in bed feeling like someone had reached inside of me and literally pulled out my organs. The pain of knowing that a part of your negligence as a parent could have contributed unwittingly to your child's pain is more unbearable than words can even describe. My deficiency was that I did not know myself, nor had I escaped from the impact of my past when I became a parent.

Her words were repetitive in saying that I did not care about her. I would argue this position endlessly with her, but the truth that I was unaware of was that I did not care about myself, so how could I adequately display concerned for her?

I did not like myself based on my past and I wanted her to be a reflection of what I did not think I could be internally. I pushed her to be the best Christian on the planet, with no mercy. She had to be better! Typically, as parents we desire our children to be better than us, but she had to be without a mistake and perfect so she could be acceptable to my family. She had to be acceptable, so the broken, scared, traumatized little girl within me could be acceptable to herself and to the world. I convinced myself that this was for her, but secretly, this was for me. Again, I was seeking to fill my need of acceptance with my family—a family I was so fearful of losing and a family that had abandoned me emotionally. It does not make sense retrospectively, but while you exist in unhealthy thinking and living, you are often unaware of the truth or the damage from the result of your actions.

My guilt was not only due to my failures, in my estimation, as a mother, but from the trauma of the past. I believed that somehow I was at fault for my childhood abuse, which led to my non-forgiveness of myself for not speaking up after the first abuse encounter.

The process of *Coming Out* of my guilt took place as I participated in a support group, which pushed me to practice more personal reflection and personal accountability. During the support group, I completed an exercise to describe how I harmed myself and others. This exercise was a powerful experience of awareness as I stood face to face with my actions and the impact of my actions. There was no place to run from me. Observing in writing and reading aloud to a trusted friend how I harmed myself and others presented me with a choice. I could choose to learn from this experience and information (wisdom), or I could choose to stand still with this emotional stronghold of guilt and non-forgiveness.

Reflective and retrospective analysis revealed the misplaced guilt from my childhood trauma and the guilt I held as a mother. The guilt, much like the shame, manifested in my physical body and felt like a fifty-pound weight sitting on my shoulders. I could not seem to lift the guilt as I witnessed my daughter's daily agony from her trauma; as well as, constantly ruminated on the fact that I did not protect her from the hands of religious people who her hurt deeply. I witnessed her agony from suffering through my emotional instability and suicidal contemplations. There was no place for me to run from her pain and loss, or from my pain and loss.

Coming Out!

A Secret Hope

At some point, my guilt, fear, and non-forgiveness fostered mental distress, depression, and I questioned my mental health survival. Under the despair was a sincere desire to stop living in the dark place of guilt and non-forgiveness. Furthermore, I desperately desired to repair my relationship with my daughter and carried a quiet hope that our relationship could heal. With that secret hope and faith in God, even at the darkest moments, I pushed myself to travail, despite the setbacks in our relationship!

Coming Out of guilt and non-forgiveness comes from a simple desire and the will of the person! There is power when a glimmer of hope remains within you! Gratitude can be the response for the possession of this internal hope that allows us to fight for ourselves!

> **There is power when a glimmer of hope remains within you!**

I decided to embark on a simple but powerful activity. I began standing in front of my mirror, looking at myself and speaking to my inner child, my teenage self, my young adult self, and my present-day self and repeating these words, "Lisa, I forgive you. Lisa, I forgive the young girl who did not know how to tell an adult about the abuse. Lisa, I forgive the teenage girl who did not tell her mom about her sexual violations. Lisa, I forgive the young adult woman and adult woman who made poor choices for herself. Lisa, I forgive the woman who did not trust herself, who sought to please others, who sacrificed herself for the sake of her family, who did not reveal her real pain so others could have been aware of it. Lisa, I forgive you as a mother, who neglected your daughter emotionally, who only knew how to love without compassion, who was abusive and overly critical, who did not get to know her daughter, who parented out of fear and who did the best that she knew how to do."

The practice of speaking audibly to yourself is a powerful tool to release guilt and unshackle non-forgiveness. According to a *John Hopkins Medicine* article, "Forgiveness, Your Health Depends on It," research indicates the action of forgiving has positive benefits for you physiologically and is preventative for cardiac issues and the reduction of mental health issues. [6] Learning to forgive is a participatory process of continually electing to release the hostile emotions against the offender, regardless of their worth. [6] *Coming Out* of non-forgiveness and guilt does have an element of forgiveness for those who have offended you, but the major offender who needs this manner of forgiveness is you!

Steps to guide you in releasing guilt and gaining acceptance of personal forgiveness:

- ~ Acceptance to the harm you have caused yourself and others.
- ~ Make the choice to forgive yourself. This is an active and intentional choice.
- ~ Stop punishing yourself for the harm you caused you or others. Keep in mind you cannot change the past.
- ~ Acknowledge that you do have the power to reframe your thinking about guilt and forgiveness, but it will take work and support. One strategy is to employ the practice of asking yourself, "What would you tell your friend who was struggling with forgiveness?" Would you be kind and more patient with her/him? Well, consider extending the same advice and mercy to yourself.

- ~ Visualization exercises such as taking your guilt and non-forgiveness to a place where it can be washed away.
- ~ Utilize prayer and mindfulness.
- ~ Incorporate regular exercise to release any physical tension.
- ~ Practice audible forgiveness exercises.
- ~ Learn how to be emotionally supportive, if you can make amends for your mistakes as a parent, especially if it caused undue stress to your children. It could be asking your children for forgiveness. It could be taking responsibility when you ignored the truth of your poor choices or words or deeds with your children.

Defensiveness becomes less prominent as you are not reacting to your guilt and the lack of personal forgiveness. You begin to live in acceptance and in the present moment verses focusing all of your energy on past hurts or failures. *Coming Out* of guilt and non-forgiveness affords you freedom within your spirit.

8

Coming Out of Unhealthy Relationships

Cracks in the surface…
Here I was, an accomplished, polished, professional African-American woman with a strong personality and sassy attitude! However, I had a secret … my secret was that I was extremely controlling and rigid with everyone around me, but I really did not have any appropriate boundaries in my relationships. I people pleased; I manipulated others; I subjected myself to manipulation by others that I trusted to easily; I hid behind an image because I feared that if anyone really saw me… that those persons would not accept me.

I always marveled at how people in my life viewed me to be such a strong individual, but what they saw was a person operating from a survivalist strength mentality. I was not a person with maturing strength in all areas of my life; however, I lived under a pretense of strength for many years. Yet, I was unaware I had cracks in my surface. The fearful, insecure woman with poor boundaries was seeping out of me in my personal and professional life.

Coming Out!

Facing My Unhealthiness

Another painful insight in my life was admitting that I was unhealthy. Since I was unhealthy, I had to conclude that some of my relationships fell under this umbrella as well. Unawareness of your unhealthiness is like being in a dark room, but you think that you are in a room with brilliant lighting accompanied by crystal chandeliers illuminating rays of light from every angle. This skewed view allows your awareness to be minimal as you continue in denial and fail to operate in your fullest integrity.

Earlier in the book, I shared that a family friend asked me to examine myself as it related to my divorce with my ex-husband. So after several years of personal work and personal crashes, severe relational challenges with my daughter, traumatic experiences from my childhood, a severely destructive and evil experience in a church cult, I had to ask myself what was wrong with me. After therapy, self-help books, spiritual work, prayer, trying different disciplines, and unawareness of my denials, I had to ask myself what was wrong with me.

By divine guidance, I attended a life coach certification where I heard about an author, Pia Mellody, who wrote the book, *Facing Codependency* [7]. I believe that God orchestrated this experience as I was searching desperately for a solution to address my internal questions. After purchasing the book, reading, and answering the questions, I came to the recognition that I possessed co-dependent thinking and behaviors. I felt a major relief and excitement as I was able to find some tools to assist me with my unhealthy relationships, particularly the unhealthy relationship I possessed with myself.

All of my unhealthy relationships came from the following: a) I did not know myself; b) I did not trust myself; c) I had unmet needs due to an unawareness of myself; d) my abuse history; e) my family dynamic;

and f) the fear of losing my family based on my foster care experience. Additionally, I had not completed my reflective and retrospective analysis, reconnected to my emotions, nor fully recognized my power to activate The Four-A's Principle in my life.

> **You have to come to this truth, if you are truly safe from the harmful environment ... you are safe, and you can now trust that you are safe!**

Coming Out may help you recognize the hidden agenda you have for your relationships. Most people come into a relationship with an unspoken need or agenda and seek fulfillment or wholeness by the others person's presence in their lives. However, when you begin to honor yourself, the question becomes, "Does the relationship in its current state feed or speak to my hidden agenda? We have to be honest with ourselves if this is the case. The key is when we articulate what we want or need from a relationship that we are mindful that the need or desire we seek to fulfill originates with our relationship with ourselves first.

I did not fully understand my hidden agendas until my late-40s. Due to sacrificing myself for the acceptance of my family and unawareness of my personal needs, I comprehended that my relationship with my family promoted a protective mode. This protection mode manifested as control, manipulation, a false sense of self, and a consistent readiness for a battle. In order to get healthy, I understood I needed to turn off this element of myself so I could turn on compassion. However, this exercise required that I distanced myself from my family for a while and learn new skills for my relationships.

Coming Out!

One of the key thinking errors that I had to shift related to the reality that I was NOW safe! Oftentimes, if safety is foreign and chaos is prevalent, you tend to develop a mechanism to keep yourself safe. You have to come to this truth, if you are truly safe from the harmful environment ... you are safe, and you can now trust that you are safe!

I used to think that the only way to reveal myself would be by showing my true qualities through my family—qualities like caring and supporting my family members in need, making sure it was evident how much I loved my mother, touting my family accomplishments every time I could. This was where I saw my worth, not as an individual but attached to my family. It was vital to protect my family and my family name. If I was protecting my family name, unconsciously I was protecting myself. To the converse, if I was touting my family, I was subconsciously lifting myself up.

Putting distance from unhealthy systems allows you to recognize your value as an individual, and it allows you to recognize that being true to who you are is more than enough! Your family plays a great role in your life but it should not be to your detriment. Learning to practice the "Four A's Principle" and moving through the *Coming Out* process matters! It is important to come out of unhealthy relationships and start new ones.

Here is the deal: I love my family and my family loves me in the capacity of how they love. However, I needed to discover myself outside of my family's triumphs and pitfalls. I needed to stand alone in my own being, so I could learn myself and create boundaries on what was best for my life, not what was best for my family only. Creating boundaries and healthiness with my family meant I accepted that I only controlled myself and the energies I invite into my life. Further, in order to honor my boundaries, some of my family associations would no longer exist, so that my mental health and well-being remained a priority.

Unhealthy Relationship with Motherhood

Since I was completely unaware of my unhealthy relationships, I became a mother who transferred the worth I perceived to receive from my family to the worth I perceived that I received from my daughter. The problem came when she wanted to be a human and not my robot. She did normal things like make mistakes, and disappoint me, but I was so unhealthy that I became angry. I took her actions as an affront to me! The more she wanted to express her individuality, the more I sought to control and manipulate so she could be what I needed her to be, not what or whom she was destined to be.

Going into parenthood, I was not ready to love my daughter in a healthy way, which is why I believe individuals whom seek to become a parent should work on being their best self, prior to parentage, if possible. If not, when you become aware of your unhealthiness, I would hope it leads you to your *Coming Out* experience.

On my journey, I grasped that I got my sense of esteem by others' views of me and my accomplishments in life. This meant if my daughter was not living up to some invisible standard that I created, then I failed, and she suffered. I struggled to bring myself to a healthy equilibrium for many years due to this faulty view of self.

Getting Support Matters

One of the best decisions I made for myself was to attend a free co-dependent anonymous support group. I am a licensed clinician, so I entered this environment with great trepidation because I was not familiar with this group framework. Additionally, after being in a church cult, I was afraid and resistant to anything that brought conformity to someone's view.

Coming Out!

However, here is what I experience at this group:

- ~ Commonality – I observed other professional, non-professionals, regular people, just like myself, sharing their desire for healthy relationships and their experiences in unhealthy relationships.
- ~ Judgement Free Zone – A place where I could be completely honest without judgment. This was something I never experienced before, and it was refreshing.
- ~ Voices Heard – A place where my voice was heard because the premise of the group was active listening and not to speak while someone else is speaking.
- ~ Self-Awareness – A place where I could further observe and learn about unhealthy thinking, behaviors, and relationships.
- ~ Self-Care – A place that I further fostered my need to take care of myself.
- ~ Integrity – A place where I could finally tell the truth—the good, bad and the ugly. It is a great feeling to release the years of garbage that I emotionally carried and that caused so much personal damage to my psyche.

In your *Coming Out* process, attending this type of support group may be useful for you. I encourage you to find a place to grow your awareness with a climate that breeds personal acknowledgement, that promotes your acceptance, and pushes your action for transformation. I started writing this book on my *Coming Out* approximately two years before attending the support group. However, my experience within the support group taught me skills and provided insights that was necessary for me to finish writing this book. My *Coming Out* blueprint can be the birthplace for you to come out of spaces where you are stuck in your life.

Some steps to improve your unhealthy relationships:

- ~ Start with yourself. The first relationship that needs repairing is the one with you.
- ~ Do you know your needs? Try a Needs Assessment.
- ~ Examine your boundaries – Are your boundaries good, bad, or non-existent?
- ~ Participate in activities to learn your needs and boundaries.
- ~ Analyze your environment – Is it healthy or conducive to develop healthy boundaries for yourself and others?
- ~ Reclaim your authentic voice through fully realizing your identity and accepting that who you are is more than enough. Acceptance can allow further awareness to grow.
- ~ Seek to reject any thoughts that suggest learning additional personal growth areas as a negative awareness. Growth = transformation ... like the caterpillar changes to a butterfly.
- ~ Open the opportunity for your uniqueness, your beauty, and your individuality to emerge, so when you look in the mirror, your truest self is reflecting back at you.
- ~ Speak with your authentic voice and be your authentic self.

Changing your internal script is a physical and active process. As I practiced positive affirmations, there was a physical reaction to not wanting to let go of the negative energy and my default internal script. You must fight diligently to push beyond your feelings and negative self-talk to learn new ways to communicate internally to yourself.

You must mourn the part of you that wants unhealthiness and negative energy to abide in your life.

Analyze the incoming data. When others communicate to you, ask yourself how you interpreting incoming data? Is it skewed from past abuse, trauma, or hurt only? Can you allow yourself to take incoming data from a positive frame? This can be done by starting with positive affirmations and saying what is actually happening verses what we perceive is happening. This is possible simply by asking a person for clarity. Like, when you said that were you joking or complimenting me? Let them answer before you judge the data and then chose to accept that truth and give yourself permission to respond in a positive and healthy way for you.

Broken relationships – determine if amends is necessary, but if the relationship has run its course in your life, cut the invisible cord that holds you to another person so development of yourself and strength can begin to bloom.

If the relationship that needs amends is with your child, you can start with the following actions:

- ~ Admit to yourself where you caused the little child who needed you pain.
- ~ Go to your child and acknowledge the error or mistake, ask your child for forgiveness, and tell your child as you fight yourself, you will also fight for him/her.
- ~ Acknowledge that your neglect left your child scared, alone, and in need.
- ~ Tell your child the truth that you did what you thought was right, but you were unaware your choices caused so much damage. Explain that you wished you had been self-aware and supportive.
- ~ Commit to learning new skills to improve yourself and then repair the parent/child relationship.

~ Look for indicators that reveal you are recreating unhealthy relationships and immediately take accountability to interrupt this pattern.

Remember, in the *Coming Out* process, you will have to confront your default programming. As a reminder, default programming is the thinking and behavior patterns you have been operating from before you started your self-awareness journey and this *Coming Out* process to learn new skills. Your default programming is driven from your past disappointments, anger, pain, and avoidant coping skills. Our default programming triggers default thinking, default emotional reactions, and default behaviors. However, the goal today is constant conscientiousness of the manifestations of default programming and to counteract the negative by learning healthier thinking and behavioral patterns.

9

Coming Out of Anger

Why are you always frowning? This is a question my brother asked me when I was in high school. The funny thing is that I was completely unaware I was frowning. I had no idea my internal emotions were noticeable on my face. As I look back and analyze myself, I believe my frown was my silent plea for anyone to see my pain … to see my anger. As a teenager, my feelings were far from my awareness, but that frown represented a clue to the rage I carried for years.

Merriam Webster's online dictionary defines "anger" as a noun describing "a strong feeling of displeasure and usually of antagonism" or "rage." Further, anger is defined as a verb described as making (someone) angry or becoming angry. [10] Both definitions of anger applied to my personality and me as a person.

Anger was my drug of choice!

Some people shop to relieve stress, some people exercise to channel their energy, some may pray or meditate to usher in balance. While others may drink or use food to cope, I chose anger! Anger was my drug of choice! It was my vice and this habit developed early in my life as I described the frown that painted my face as a teen. Anger did not become my weapon until I could see myself in power or in control. In my adulthood, I began to develop a strategic method to use my anger in dangerous and toxic ways.

Anger's Power Play

Anger played out in my reactions to others as defensiveness, sarcasm, and passive aggressiveness. When I perceived that someone hurt me, I commenced a private campaign to rally others to go against the person who offended me. Secretly, this was a win for me: particularly if my campaign resulted in those persons being in agreement with me.

Anger played out in my ability to tell someone off or critically cut him or her down without raising my voice—a harmful choice of power that I partook in verses learning to be honest with my feelings.

I did not know how to express hurt, loneliness, fear, nervousness, or any other emotions other than anger. The sad part about my anger … is that after hurting someone, I secretly felt good. At times, I held a smirk on my face in a diabolical manner because I enjoyed my anger and its impact. Anger fed my soul, and I had a damaged soul.

I am confident that I would not have dealt with my anger, if I did not become a mother. Sadly, my child suffered at the hands of my anger the most. I lost myself in my anger as I parented my daughter. I recall times when she pleaded for her mom. For her, that woman who was unleashing this anger on her was not her mother. She did not have a means to escape my world of unhealed madness and the environment of rage that seeped out from my pores on a daily basis.

Through therapy, self-reflection, prayer, and retrospective analysis, I discovered that shame was the root cause of my anger. Here I was … a beautiful, spiritual being that allowed victimhood to direct my anger, guilt, and shame! A very simple question to unlock the caustic agreements that I made with anger was, "Why am I angry?"

As I answered this question reflectively, I conjured the following answers:

- ~ Unresolved pain from childhood abuse.
- ~ The creation of a fantasy for my life and my real life did not match.
- ~ Single mom struggles…lack financial and paternal support from my daughter's father.
- ~ Lack of emotional support without a learned method to ask for help or support for myself.
- ~ Lack of self-esteem.
- ~ Non-forgiveness.
- ~ Denial of feelings.
- ~ Not speaking from my authentic voice.
- ~ Shame.

There is so much more that I could share about how I exhibited anger in my life, but what is valuable now is *Coming Out* of anger.

One of the first components is to develop self-awareness regarding how uncontrolled anger is creating unhealthy cognitions and behaviors within you, as well as harming others.

Your awareness can occur, but it requires honesty, the sense of personal safety, and whether you will choose to remove the blinders to tell yourself the truth! It will take humility to actualize your truth, and then you must communicate within you and pronounce openly that you have taken anger too far. During your awareness process, honesty will propel more awareness in your mind and life. It is necessary to ask a very simple question of, "Why am I angry?"

A second component of the process, as the awareness grows, is your willingness to admit what you are learning about yourself. <u>The truth is the truth!</u> What you learn about your thinking and behaviors does not mean this is the core you, but it is whom you have merged into based on your past and those unhealthy agreements.

- ~ Admit you have been denying aspects of your life to yourself.
- ~ Admit you could have an addiction to anger.
- ~ Accept your allowance to let anger morph into your emotional crutch of manipulative and destructive actions.

In my process of admission and acceptance of my love affair with anger, I researched my default programming of anger and my abuse cycle.

Coming Out!

My Abuse Cycle

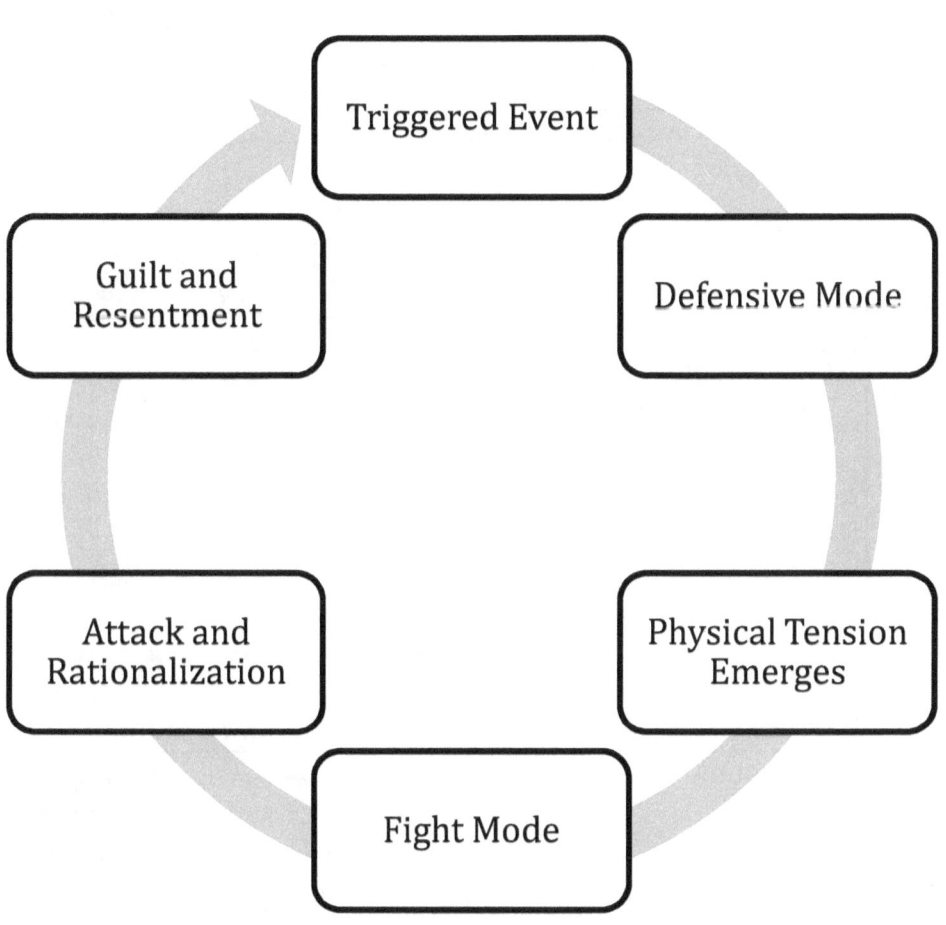

My Abuse Cycle Internal and External Manifestations

Triggered Event	~ Not feeling safe ~ Perceiving that I am being controlled ~ Perceiving that I am being put down/criticized
Defensive Mode	~ My internal self-talk seeks to tell me that I am safe ~ Starting to interrupt the speaker ~ Stop hearing what is being said because I am working on not overreacting
Physical Tension Emerges	~ Start moving or fidgeting ~ Start to focus on something other what is being spoken ~ Fighting hard internally not to shut down ~ Asking for a way out of the interaction in a poor manner (making an excuse to finish the discussion at a later time) ~ Informing the other party that I don't want to talk or need a break
Fight Mode	~ Going for the kill to get out of the interaction…I don't care if I harm you now because I perceive you are attacking me ~ Not feeling safe ~ Walking out ~ Over talking you to shut you down ~ Making you feel like the problem

Attack and Rationalization	~ *No longer able to remain in the present* ~ *Dissociating to a cold, anger armor* ~ *Physical anxiety is high* ~ *Don't' feel heard and getting angrier and afraid because I am feeling controlled and unsafe*
Guilt and Resentment	~ *Tell myself that I was not wrong or the other person is overacting* ~ *Angry that this person upset me* ~ *Within twenty-four hours, feeling bad and guilty, starting to punish myself for hurting the person* ~ *Will offer an apology, but may not mean it* ~ *Cry and really try to change*

A third component takes you to the reflective and retrospective analysis, which can assist in your identification of the harm caused to yourself and others. It is critical at this stage to take the time to list the harm imposed to you and others in your life. Recognize that the first person you harm is yourself, and typically those whom are the closest to you.

A fourth component must be acknowledgement and forgiveness. Acknowledge the harm, make peace with your behaviors, and seek self–forgiveness. Make a list of the benefits of forgiveness to yourself. It could be healthier relationships, improved mental health, less anxiety, stress or hostility, lower blood pressure, fewer episodes of depression, or improved esteem. Your benefits of forgiveness will be conducive and personal to you.

A fifth component can be to make amends for your anger and its consequences. Amends is a simple act of making up for wrongdoing. This can take on many forms. The optimal time to deploy amend efforts are when you are seeking self-growth. This means that you cannot control the other person's reaction to your efforts to make amends. The person may or may not be ready to accept your action to make amends, and you have to accept it. In some cases, making amends may be harmful and this requires good awareness of the relationship dynamic.

A sixth component will be to learn new skills through self-help, therapy, counseling, and/or support groups. Having accountability for your relationship with anger is vital for recovery from this toxic activity in your life.

A significant realization for you will be to understand that your abuse cycle could be primarily internal not external. Meaning that you are not walking around attacking others, you are walking around attacking yourself! How can this be? If you have lack of esteem, unfulfilled potential, rapid fire negative self-talk plaguing you from past hurts and experiences, or you have made agreements with unhealthy messages in your psyche, <u>YOU</u> could be the bigger abuser in your life! Facing yourself is a scary thing because you are focused on the other person, people, or experiences that you may be unconsciously using to punish yourself with your inward anger.

Inward anger could be taking the blame in a situation, when blame is not warranted, thus producing guilt or resentment.

Inward anger could be adopting the notion that you did something wrong and now you should punish yourself by telling yourself that you are not good enough, bad, not worthy or deserving of compassion, love, peace, joy, happiness, or forgiveness.

Inward anger could be participating in activities that are harmful for you … from unprotected sex to eating disorders.

Inward anger could be allowing your mind to curse you out and treat you unkindly.

Meaning that you are not walking around attacking others, you are walking around attacking yourself.

Your inward anger will look different for you, but the key for understanding the process of *Coming Out* of anger is self-awareness. Ask yourself, the following questions, "Am I starting to punish myself?" then ask yourself, "Am I punishing myself right now?" Have you chosen to punish yourself so you would not punish others? This was one of my guilty pleasures of anger! As I mentioned previously, allowing myself to be around my abuser during my adult years when I had a choice not to be was a form of self-punishment and inward anger.

Determine within yourself that self-sacrifices are no longer worth it and create a force field of strength to move you to the next level. Creating a force field of strength encompasses finding a support system to be your wall to lean on until your personal strength is fortified. Research and learn what you need and what your boundaries should be with yourself and others. Identify your triggers and work on your internal thoughts to counteract your default programming of self-punishment and inward anger. Utilize the various tools available via books, counseling, life coaching, support groups, and/or accountability relationships. Keep practicing everyday so your default programming is framing positive and healthy choices for your anger.

Taking Control of Root Thinking-Preventing a Defensive Reaction

Here is an example of my steps to take control over root thinking and not allow my defensiveness to produce anger:

Recognize I am feeling unlovable, unworthy, or judged. Quickly own that this was my negative root thinking.

- Notice and acknowledge the physical tension because I was accepting my choice to be a victim. Have personal accountability for giving your power over to negative root thoughts.
- Be aware of my body tension or reaction. Accept what my body is saying to me regarding my negative root thoughts and physical tension. I am overreacting based on unhealthy agreements.
- Forgive myself for reacting as a victim. In the moment, immediately forgive myself and release the power of the negativity and tension.
- CHOOSE to see myself as worthy, lovable, and not judged by myself.
- Make a choice in my reaction from this truth. Now I can change my behavior from defensiveness and anger to a calm, peaceful reaction, and remain present in the conversation.

Personal Coming Out Journey Work
Recognition of the Power of Your Voice and Your Strength ~ Acknowledgement

Each of us can learn more about ourselves and through the *Coming Out* process. However, an unwillingness to acknowledge the truth and accept it impacts our growth. As you move to willingness, the *Coming Out* experience is there for you to come to self-honor, freedom, personal power, transformation, and growth!

The Serenity Prayer

"God grant me the serenity to accept the things that I cannot change, the courage to change the things that I can and wisdom to know the difference."

Serenity = the state of being calm, peaceful, and untroubled

Acceptance = the action of consenting to receive or undertake something offered

Courage = the ability to do something that frightens one

Wisdom = the quality of having experience, knowledge, and good judgment

Coming Out!

Take the time to write the Serenity Prayer in your own words as you seek acknowledgement and acceptance from God and/or from your personal power.

_____

_____
_____
_____
_____
_____
_____
_____
_____
_____
_____
_____
_____
_____
_____
_____
_____
_____
_____
_____
_____

Acknowledgment Begins with…

Acknowledge the totality of you, your history, your thoughts, your drive, and yourself in the present day.

Acknowledge that you can exist with a state of being calm, peaceful, and untroubled.

Acknowledgement means you tell the truth about what is right in front of you.

Acknowledge the fantasies that have captured your mind about you.

Acknowledge the strengths and abilities that are true about you.

Acknowledge you are worthy of love, honor, choice, value, self-care, protection, and growth.

Acknowledge any faulty thinking that could be hindering your growth.

Acknowledge that life can shift, if you allow it.

Acknowledge any mistruths that you have adapted to prevent seeing the truth in your life.

Acknowledge your humanity means you are able to grow and become stronger.

Coming Out!

ACKNOWLEDGMENT CHART
(based on empirical evidence)
Use the chart below to create your own Acknowledgement Chart.

Who are you?	Empirical evidence that supports this truth —what is the evidence/why does the evidence support this truth?	What you tell yourself.	What is true?
1.			
2.			
3.			
4.			
5.			

Acceptance begins with...

Accepting the path forward is not without fear, but with fear and courageous energy.

Accepting that you possess the courage to really see yourself as you are and where you can go.

Accepting that the truth in front of you is what it is; do not rationalize it to something else.

Accepting you now have the power to evaluate this truth; why it is true based on the experiences and/or empirical evidence.

Accepting that you can now actualize good judgment and make a different choice based on what you know about yourself today.

Accepting if you harm yourself or others based on this acknowledgement, and if possible, seek to make amends (if not harmful for you or the other person).

Accepting that you can live in your truth and it will not break you, but the truth will give you strength.

Acceptance of your power to shift your life.

Acceptance that your mistruths will have to be redefined for forward movement in your life.

Acceptance of your humanity means you are able to grow and become stronger.

Coming Out!

ACKNOWLEDGMENT and ACCEPTANCE CHART
(based on empirical evidence)

Use the chart below to create your own Acknowledgment & Acceptance Chart.

Who are you?	Empirical evidence that supports this truth –what is the evidence/why does the evidence support this truth?	What you tell yourself.	What is true?	Can I accept this truth about myself? (yes/no)	What choices do I have or can I make now with this truth?
1.					
2.					
3.					
4.					
5.					

Coming Out of Shame... You must decide to share when you are ready. Questions to ask:

- ~ Do I feel as if I have a muzzle on my mouth regarding the abuse?
- ~ How do I decide when I am ready to share?
- ~ When do I share with a trusted friend, or a support group, or a mental health professional?
- ~ Have I found a mental health professional that is the correct fit for me?
- ~ Do I have a solid support system outside of my mental health environment?

Shame Reveal Exercise: Write out in narrative form or use a pictorial diagram to reveal how shame is playing out in your life.

Use your creative skills.
Record a story that illustrates the umbrella of shame in your life.
Analyze what your narrative, pictorial diagram, or narration reveals.

Notice if you give yourself a method to escape from your shame or if you are remaining in your shame. This will be a clue regarding your readiness to share or pursue the dialogue within the context of your mental health environment.

Coming Out of Victim Mentality... You must decide if freedom is worth it.
Questions to ask:

- ~ Are you able to relate to this section of the book?

- Answer honestly if reading this section created any tension for you?
- Did you notice any resistance or anxiety as you read about victim mentality?
- Can you describe areas in your life where you are operating as a victim based on your past trauma?

<u>What Are My Needs Exercise:</u> Complete the exercise regarding discovering your needs.

This can be a tell-tale of what drives some of your victim mentality and a way to find healthier needs. *The Secret Laws of Attraction* by Talane Miedaner is an excellent resource for assessing your emotional needs. [21]

What are the actions that can be implemented to *Coming Out* of a victim mentality?

1. Create a revelation/vision –

2. Imagine what your life would look like if you did not operate from a victim mentality.

3. Learn your default thinking and behaviors (this will help you identify when you are operating in victim mentality).

4. Describe this image in pictorial terms (draw or get images to gain a visual view of your revelation).

5. Use your personal power to implement your pictorial revelation into practice.

6. Determine which steps you will take first in the revelation plan.

7. This could include a morning routine with meditation and affirmations.

8. This could include personal notes or quotes placed on your mirror and/or around your home.

9. This could include a personal message that you record on your phone to play to yourself four times a day.

10. Take action of what you decide to do for yourself.

11. Incorporate support partners – a trusted friend, a life coach, or a therapist/counselor.

Coming Out!

Coming Out of Guilt and Non-forgiveness

<u>Guilt/Forgiveness Exercise:</u> Use the face image and comment balloons to enter your thoughts of guilt and non-forgiveness.

<u>Guilt/Forgiveness Exercise Cont'd:</u> Now, if you could release the guilt and non-forgiveness thoughts, fill the comment balloons with whatever thoughts would remain in your mind.

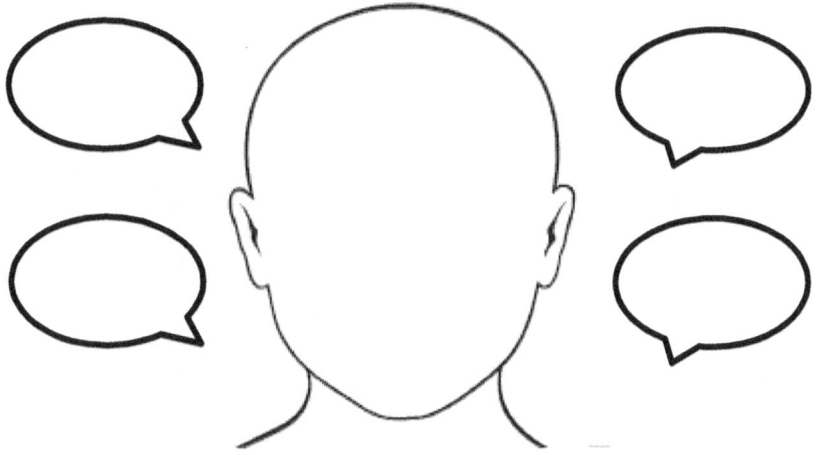

Learning to forgive is a participatory process of continually electing to release the hostile emotions against the offender (or yourself), regardless of their worth. [6]

Write down what actions you would need to take to move forward with forgiveness and *Coming Out* of guilt.

Section 4
Reclaim Your Authentic Voice and Personal Power for Positive and Healthy Ways of Living

10

Coming to Self-Love and Self-Acceptance

When you have experienced abuse in your life or unhealthy relationships from your childhood or as an adult, you believe that love costs, love hurts, and love allows instability. The truth is… Love is free! Healthy Love does not abuse! Healthy Love does not promote chaos! If you ever wonder why a random person can extend these words to you, "I love you." It is because love is freely given, and authentic love flows with no expectations when it is healthy. The one whom freely gives love understands their outpouring will come back to them just as freely as they gave it. As with God, he gives love unconditionally, without expectations, and each day we are recipients of this love… He just gives it!

On your journey to *Coming Out*, you will come to comprehend that if I am coming out of something, it means that I have an opportunity of *Coming To* something! Coming to the opportunity to make choices for personal growth, healing, acceptance, freedom and more, if we are walking in our power!? The chosen path of health and betterment will be our lifelong quest for continued growth and transformation.

Coming Out!

There must be a REAL pursuit to love you! Loving yourself is not a new concept as this concept has been stated many times before by speakers, psychologists, and counselors.

However, the responsibility to make a choice to love ourselves is more than a concept; it must become our daily reality. It is vital to recognize when God reveals or ordinary people speak to you and communicate to you to start loving yourself that you follow the prompting.

A while ago as I was doing my meditation and positive affirmations, I listened to the speaker articulate those three simple words, "I love you." She did not know me, but she was willing to freely express her love to me without expectations because she was speaking to me through a recorded audiobook. It was a momentous instance that I allowed my spirit, body, and mind to accept her gift and I chose to tell myself, "Lisa, I do love you!" Outside of speaking internally to myself, I needed to communicate aloud to myself every day those words, "Lisa, I love you!" Within the same week, I listened to an author who was sharing on a television program mention a thirty-day I love you challenge. I knew that I was operating in the world of God's plan for me! The universe was presenting an opening for me to walk into, or should I say to "Come to self-love and self-acceptance," and I was not going to walk past this door!

Dare to Accept Love

It is imperative that you stand before yourself and speak to every phase of life to convey to that person your unconditional love.

I set forth to speak to a little girl whom was hurting from childhood trauma!

> **There must be a REAL pursuit to love you!**

I set forth to speak to the teenager who sought love through relationships with men!

I set forth to speak to the young adult woman who searched desperately for others to approve of her.

I set forth to speak to the adult woman who was fighting for her soul to be peaceful and healthy and to be present in her life.

Choosing to love all of those people that represented my life was the gateway to *Coming Out* of and *Coming To* my journey for personal life impact.

Starting the practice of this love is outlined in our previous chapters and in the *Four A's Principle*: The picture of this process could be the following: a possession of an awareness that you lack self-love, an acknowledgment of your need for self-love, an acceptance of where you are in your life and that you are not loving that aspect of yourself, and then moving into action of the practice self-love.

Your internal actions are ongoing and continual. It is combat! You must recognize that you are up against years of not loving you and those messages. You are up against your default programming and even people who are equally unhealthy who are in your life. Communicate to yourself how much you love you. Make time to learn yourself and your needs. Be able to identify and shift the internal messages to something that looks like love. Be honest with yourself. Choose to accept it despite what your default programming tells you. If you have a bad day, don't quit on you! Continue to this practice each day going forward the rest of your life.

Your external actions are ongoing but require discipline. Verbally tell yourself that you love each part of you that felt unloved—the little child, teenager, the young adult, and your present-day self. Stand in the mirror and look into your eyes and soul. Continue until your mind, body, and spirit align and your conscience allows this gift. Push against your inner thoughts to receive your own words. Remind yourself with post-it notes around your home, car, or at work. Ask your friend, a family member, or a partner to write you a letter expressing their love for you.

In healing and the *Coming To* process, it is essential to receive the love that is all around us, and to receive love from ourselves. Your desire to live at a higher loving state requires increasing self-love and your capacity to accept, give, and receive love. The truth is... *Love is free! Love is spiritual! Love has to be nurtured! Love is unconditional! Love is concerned for the well-being of others! Ultimately, love comes from God, but the question is: Will you accept His love?*

The action of self-love can begin with some fundamental questions such as:

What is love?
What is self-love?
What would self-love look like for me?
What is my internal script about self-love?
What are my external manifestations based on my lack of self-love?
Self-love equals self-care. Where do you need self-care?

When you love yourself, you do not tend to neglect yourself. You take care of your mind, body, and spirit. Find and incorporate a discipline in your life that promotes self-care, such as:

~ Meditation
~ Mindfulness
~ Exercise
~ Prayer
~ Pleasurable activities that commences happiness in a healthy way
~ Hobbies that you enjoy
~ Regular medical check-ups

Self-love assists in understanding your needs. As you discover yourself further in the *Coming Out* process, you want to establish your needs and boundaries. This process may seem overwhelming, so I am a big proponent of using the resources that are available to us. One book that I found helpful for my process of understanding my needs was *The Secret Laws of Attraction* by Talane Miedaner. [21] You can fail at loving yourself, if you are mistaken of your needs. Healthy love equals identifying yourself completely.

Self-love is refuting negative agreements with the truth!

Self-Acceptance

Self-acceptance will be the natural fall-out of embracing self-love. On my journey to my authentic truth, I had to reconcile with the person that I am presenting to the world and the person that I am. In my late 40s, I recognized that I had become accustomed to living in dualities. I think living in duality of worlds is very common for a person of color in America because there are certain American standards that we are all supposed to ascribe to for assimilation. For example, in America, we are taught and required to speak the English language, but if you are person of color, you may speak a different language or style while at home. However, living in duality of worlds between you verses whom you are pretending to be is different based on the motivation. If your motivations are rooted in unhealthy thinking and behaviors, you will live in a daily contradiction of yourself. I was seeking alignment for myself due to a lack of self-acceptance, a lack of self-identity, and a lack of self-esteem.

Awareness of who you are, and awareness of your needs can take you to acknowledging that you may need to build your esteem. *Coming To* your authentic truth requires fortifying your personal core with the truth of who you are, and that commences with the following:

Self-love commences with totally understanding what this entails for you, conceptually, and practically. This can begin with fully conceding to the love that God pours out through the universe on a daily basis. Also, with the recognition that this love is available to you if you are open to receive it.

Get to know yourself. Over the course of thirty days complete the exercise of writing one new thing that you discover about yourself via personal reflection, conversation with others or acquired information.

Reclaim your belief in yourself. Possessing faith that your personal core is good, lovable, worthy, and priceless makes a difference. Grieve and release the false view of your personal self, which was created by fear, control, deception, shame, and non-forgiveness.

Honor your life with realistic boundaries by identifying what boundaries are, classifying your personal boundaries, and creating a plan to live within them.

Create safety in your life to be yourself. It is so vital that you are comfortable in your own skin.

Accepting that you are enough and the things that must change about you are for your pleasure, your health, and your life impact.

Trust yourself by accepting that you are safe now and your thoughts are worthy of recognition.

Allow and accept your feelings.

Love is free! Love is spiritual! Love has to be nurtured! Love is unconditional! Love is concerned for the well-being of others! Ultimately, love comes from God, but the question is: Will you accept His love?

Develop your own positive affirmations and then write a summary of what those affirmations mean in practice.

My personal mantra is that each individual has an opportunity and responsibility to make life impact. I believe life impact begins with you and all the people you are blessed to interact with in your life journey.

Some steps to commence loving you:

~ Stop internal/external self-criticism! Be okay with whom you are but be free to make changes or adjustments to be healthy. You do not have to be mad to make changes. Self-acceptance allows us in our power to change and adapt, first in our thoughts, second in our actions, and third in our habits.

~ Do not terrorize yourself and do not make situations worse by creating a new movie. We do this in every area of our lives and these frightening thoughts become negative affirmations. Instead, find a positive image that aligns with the truth and when the negative thought comes up, switch to this positive image.

~ Be gentle, kind, and patient. Learn to see the mind as a garden. Select the thought you would like to create in your life, water the thought with positive energy, and a loving climate and thoughts until the created thought is one day actualized. Watch for your old negative thoughts and pluck them out quickly. Remember, it is okay to make mistakes.

~ Be kind to your mind. Self-hatred is a cancer and so you must accept that love is not earned; you exist, which means you are a vessel to receive and give love.

~ Learn the difference between responsibility and blame. Make a choice on how you will respond to the situation, and understand that blame creates guilt and seeks punishment. Consistently analyze yourself for the difference.

~ Relaxation. Allow the body to relax. Meditate. We have wisdom and the answers for our lives, and relaxation can foster spiritual awakenings and knowledge. Connecting with your inner self is a powerful tool.

> **The miracle of every day is that you can receive and accept love!**

~ Create visualizations that promote changes—images to dissolve unloving areas or images of love to manifest changes in your life.
~ Praise yourself. Tell yourself how well you are doing in every detail of your life. Allow yourself to accept the good in your life.
~ Train yourself to manage loving yourself. Questions to ask are: What do you feel love should look like in your life? Healthy or unhealthy love? Explain. Where did the answers come from for you? Are you willing to change the thought(s)?
~ Find ways to support yourself. It takes strength to ask for help.

The miracle of every day is that you can receive and accept love! Consider the exercise of sitting in your living room, dimming the lights, and scanning the room and examining all that you have in your life. Further, reflect on the positive relationships, the regular resources, your physical health, and your abilities. This assessment can allow you to embrace that you are truly loved every day. Remember, if you do not love, you only deprive yourself.

God has given us free will and each day we have the power to create the life we want. If you want a life where you believe people will hurt you and no one understands you, then you can create that life! However, if you want to take your power and create a life where anger, resentment, and blame do not run you, you have that power, and you can create that life! You may have been abused but you do not have to choose to abuse others or create a life where you still get abused—whether you abuse yourself, your mind, or your body.

It is NOW really truly up to you! Give your power to no one and stop thinking you have power over anyone but YOU! Belief in you will bring peace, love, acceptance and joy into your life and it will manifest itself! Staying stuck in past trauma only slowly kills you and you never let yourself live!

Remember, we don't get any do overs!!!

It is mind over matter; chose a different way!

Personal Journey Work
Reclaim Your Authentic Voice & Personal Power for Positive & Healthy Ways of Living

Dr. Lisa Cook, LPC, CPC

There must be a REAL pursuit to love you!

Dare to Accept Love

Love Letter to You!
A. Write a personal love letter to yourself.
B. Include all the things that you currently love about yourself and what you deserve to love about yourself.
C. Use the space below to start this love letter.

_____
_____
_____
_____
_____
_____
_____
_____
_____
_____
_____
_____
_____
_____
_____

(Use additional paper, if needed)

Coming Out!

Upon completion of your love letter, develop "I Love You Notes" from the loving words that you wrote to yourself.

Place a note out for yourself to read for at least 30 days.

Journal each day about your reaction to your love note.

Communicate each day to a safe friend expressing your love for yourself and your friend.

Section 5
Renovate Your Personal Life Vision by Forward Movement ~ Action

11

Coming Out and *Coming To* Is Ongoing and Lifelong

This period will arrive after you have experienced the success of sharing your authentic voice and walking in your power. As you are moving through the *Coming Out* process and practicing the Four-A's Principle, a new experience in life emerges, maybe a new potential relationship or a new job or a new opportunity. It will be prudent for you to prepare yourself for the reality that the *Coming Out* and the *Coming To* process is lifelong and evolutionary.

Your old default programming will want to take over and you may find yourself slipping backwards. But here is the test—do you really believe that your life is worth being healthy? If so, shifting all of the energy you used to cope from the traumatic events is necessary to fighting for yourself! Fighting to be positive! Fighting to believe the best of yourself and others! Fighting to trust that you are in control! Fighting to create your life impact! There's no time to placate the former programming, now is the time to have supportive people in your circle and a vision in action!

You have a choice in this scenario, always remember that fact! Further, you are on the other side of trauma now and you are at the stage of Post-Traumatic Growth (PTG) [19]. "PTG is the positive change experienced as a result of the struggle with a major life crisis or a traumatic event." [19] *Coming Out* is about making the personal choice for your life's positive change.

As I moved into a new relationship, I started to fall back to the negative thinking connected to my past experiences. I started to view the differences between myself and my significant other as personal rejections, which resulted in me transitioning to my protective mode. When the relationship had positive experiences, I pushed against the positive experiences, seeking to prove a different reality from my projected fears. I experienced an internal struggle that told me to use my old coping skills, hoping for different results, instead of taking a chance to use my new coping skill of communicating with my voice to shift the dynamic.

In a new relationship or a new situation, we have to give each situation a chance to play out by trusting ourselves and our power to navigate based on healthy thinking and healthy behaviors. However, as soon as you realize your relationship and/or experience is a repeat of your past relationships or experiences, make the choice to congratulate yourself for this awareness, communicate your patterns to yourself and/or your partner, communicate any actions that you would like to experience differently in the relationship or experience, and make the healthy choice to eliminate or redirect the relationship or experience if your honor and value are at stake. If it is a new relationship in your life, you must remember that the fantasy you want in the relationship is not worth the self-sacrificing of your honor and your worth. Release the relationship and trust you are deserving of what you truly believe about yourself—a great love, a reciprocal love, and respectful love! Trust your inner voice!

Stop Internal Punishment

Coming Out!

Learn to stop the internal punisher within yourself. What does this mean? It means when you have made a choice, you have to accept the positive or negative consequences of that choice, and do not start to judge yourself if the results are different from what you expected. However, if your norm is to internally start punishing yourself because the old song of self-judgment and blame is playing in your head, your mind and body is ready to be punished. Your mood will be altered because of this self-punishment and you will lash out at others or treat them rudely, coldly, or harshly because your self- imposed prison could be a manifestation of this intrinsic reaction.

Fighting for yourself is about taking on the mental exercise of evaluating your decisions, determining that you made the choice for you and not to please someone else or that you did not break a personal boundary. Accept your choice because you wanted to do what you chose to do. If you were people pleasing or you broke a personal boundary, simply accept that truth. Also, resolve internally to develop a plan to stand strong with your personal boundary, if the situation arises again, you can make a choice of personal honor and personal value. Now, go further to give yourself peace!! Offer kindness to yourself, even if someone else is offering you ridicule, and accept the kindness you are distributing and choose to grow from the experience.

Questions to ponder after your choice, as you seek strength in living in your authenticity:

~ Did I maintain my honor and value?
~ Did I compromise my values, if so, why?
~ What can I learn from this experience?

One of the things I learned about myself during the *Coming Out* process is that I can no longer rationalize things or pretend it's something different than what it really is. When I did that, I went against my core values and I did not honor myself. This may seem obvious, but let's be careful not to be prideful about ourselves when it comes to relationships. Oftentimes, our hidden agendas are operating, so we are constantly twisting ourselves like pretzels to stay within an unhealthy interaction or relationship.

Our ability to complete this type of exercise helps us become aware of the very thing we have power over ... ourselves!! We can make choices based on our awareness. Sometimes these choices are easy and sometimes they are difficult, but we can do them! We are strong enough ... because we don't have to live with fear of releasing a relationship that means we sacrificed ourselves for someone's needs if they don't honor us!

In Closing – Give Yourself a Second Chance.

As I close this book, I come to the awareness of a different species that resembles my life today. It may be cliché, but it is very applicable to the transformative experience I have engaged, and I continue to participate in daily. The butterfly captures my interest, because as I choose to honor my authentic voice, my soul transforms daily into the beauty and freedom of the butterfly.

I firmly believe that we will live in a society where authenticity to who you really are is a mystery to most of us. Really, we have been conditioned to assimilate ourselves to whatever is the trend of the masses. Cultural norms and societal expectations shape us to think it is okay not to be different in any way, so our individuality is shunned. Honoring and valuing our true selves becomes less important and diminishes its worth. The question is: Who is really willing to take the risk to be true and authentic to themselves? I believe this personal discovery makes the most life impact anyone could ever experience. From there, we can go on to touch other lives because we are true and authentic to ourselves and we participate in the *Coming Out* process.

The discovery of the spiritual being that God created you to be is well worth it! Not the person you've become because of life. *Coming Out* is also *Coming To* and it is a cyclical process. As you evolve in one area, there is a new opportunity to become more authentic and honorable to yourself in another area of your being and life. *Coming Out* of the person marked by trauma, and/or unhealthiness and to *Coming To* being in love with the beauty of whom you are as person—divinely and beautifully shaped—to create life impact is the lifelong pursuit!

As I shared my perspective with my co-worker about living in one's authenticity and the commonality of struggles that each human encounters in life, she mentioned that we should give ourselves a second chance. I agreed with her and that sentiment aligned with my journey of *Coming Out*. The reality is that I had to give myself a chance to move forward so I would not remain stuck in the darkness and pain of my past!

I practice giving myself a second chance each day.
A second chance in self-love…
A second chance in self-acceptance…
A second chance in faith…
A second chance in hope…
A second chance in embracing my emotions…
A second chance to heal…
A second chance to learn myself and walk in my power…

If you are reading this book, I am asking that you give yourself a chance.

A second chance to heal…
A second chance to redevelop your personal relationship…
A second chance to be your authentic self…
A second chance love yourself…
A second chance to live out the Four A-Principle…
A second chance to have joy…
A second chance to love others…
A second chance at happiness…
A second chance just to be perfectly, unapologetically YOU…
A second chance to *Come Out!*

12

Casting a Vision to Catapult Your Motivation Forward

It is my belief that reinventing a new personal life vision commences with the simple act of casting the vision!

"A vision is your dream." [3] It is now time to ask yourself the fundamental question of, "What is the desire for my life right now? If your desire is *Coming Out*, how differently would your life look?

Your personal voice is the pathway for you to create life impact. As you participate, you gain strength to practice forward movement.

This final chapter is about provoking your practice to exercise your personal and authentic voice. There will be a series of questions for you to reflect and analyze within yourself with someone you trust, like a friend, family member, or therapist/counselor.

Can you identify any past events or experiences that you believe are impacting your life today?

In the previous section reviews, were you able to identify themes that you feel require further exploration? Have you explored these themes with your support system (a mental health professional, a life coach, support group, or a trusted friend)? Can you outline your identified themes below?

From a historical perspective, how would you describe your emotional maturity?

Present day, how would you classify your coping skills? Please choose below and explain why you made that choice.

Active Coping [5] –

Avoidant Coping [5] –

What steps could assist you in becoming more present with your emotions in your current life?

Now that you have experienced reflective analysis, reconnected with your emotions, and recognized your voice, what do you want life to be like for your personal life impact?

Section Three covered several areas where you were able to exercise personal *Coming Out* experiences, upon reading:

- ~ Have you found any similarities?
- ~ Do you feel comfortable to choose your voice?
- ~ Do you have a support system?

~ How can you strengthen your authentic voice and honor yourself in your present life?

"A vision statement is a short phrase or sentences to articulate your hope for the future." [3]

Spiritual Vision Statement Example: Improving my energy and spiritual self by invoking my strength to practice forgiveness.

Wellness Vision Statement Example: Discover the strength of my true voice by focusing on my reflective and respective analysis.

Practice Vision Statement Example: Understanding my coping behaviors by researching active and avoidant coping, journaling my emotional reactions for thirty days, and interviewing individuals within my life cycle for the next four-weeks.

Personal Impact Map

Ask yourself the following question: "What would I like to change in my life to create my personal life impact?"

_____
_____
_____

After you are able to define your vision, then you want to outline practical actions to fulfill your vision, which is considered your personal impact map.

A personal impact map allows you to give the specific steps to see results from your vision and communicate in writing the significance of your chosen activities associated with your vision. [3]

Your desire for life impact (write your desire for life impact below)

Your vision for life impact in your life (write your vision)

Your identified steps to choose your life impact (write your steps with specific timelines)

The significance for each step identified (write why each identified step has significance for you)

Coming Out!

Life Impact Results (write the results you seek to happen or when your results have been achieved)

Operate your life impact vision to propel movement. Consider the components you need to operationalize your vision, find them, lock them in and make them happen!

Putting New Behaviors into Practice for Life Impact

"Learning to stop my default programming and responses by learning to proceed with my transformed, chosen, and intentional response."

STOP! – Here is where you STOP and step back from the situation in your mind or physically!
TAKE A BREATH – Breathe slowly, once or twice, to encourage your mind, soul and body to relax and calm itself... You may even use exercise as your time to breathe and relax. You may use meditations to relax. You may use positive affirmations to breathe, relax and refocus.
OBSERVE – Ask yourself.... What's happing in my environment, within my body, within my life right now? What am I reacting too? Has there been an emotional trigger that I am overlooking? What am I thinking and feeling? What are the words that mind is saying to me right now? Where is my focus of attention?
PULL BACK----PUT IN A POSITIVE PERSPECTIVE – Move from feelings to knowledge of what is true... Is this fact based on empirical evidence/opinion or feelings? Can I see this situation as an observer? How would an objective person view this situation? What spiritual, non-spiritual, or wise advice would I give to someone else? What meaning am I giving to this event? How important will my actions be to myself and my goal? Will there be any consequences?
PRACTICE WHAT HONORS YOU - Taking wisdom into everyday living... What can I do that will be most helpful to my spiritual and personal growth?

Coming Out!

> What can I do that will be most helpful to the spiritual and personal growth of someone else?
> Am I keeping my values and principles in my action?
> Will this choice increase my peace, love, joy or cause the opposite effect?
> Will my actions be effective and appropriate to my lifestyle and others?

Original Design-Carolyn Vivian 2010[17]/Redesigned –Dr. Lisa Cook 2019(LifeImpactCircles)

Quotes to Influence Change

Power
Keep Your Power!
The measure of one's power is connected to one's mindset and how each person filters in information.
Your power says if it rains; you will choose to look for the rainbow!
Your power says if I am experiencing disappointment, you will choose to keep hope for better times!
Your power says if I fail on the 1st, 2nd, and 3rd attempt, you will choose to continue to try and try again!
Your power says if you hurt me, you will choose to forgive for the betterment of your heart!
Powers says that believing in yourself is paramount!

Your Greatness Is Tied to Your Gratefulness
Don't let negativity of life experiences outweigh your gratitude!
Gratefulness is the feeling or demonstration of appreciation of kindness or being appreciative of benefits received in your life
Open your eyes & look around at all of your benefits!
Let go of yesterday because you cannot relive it.
Release negative tension.
Choose to intentionally promote good thoughts.
Smile, because it could be worst!

Coming Out!

Love You No Matter What

Whatever choices that you make in your day, good or bad, helpful or harmful, against your core beliefs or aligned with your values.
TELL YOURSELF, I LOVE YOU!
If your spirit rejects this truth, say it again!
If your spirit grieves this truth, say it again!
If your spirit accepts this truth, say it again!
Let nothing or no one stop you from loving yourself unconditionally!
LOVING YOU = VALUE & STRENGTH!

YOU ARE THE MISSION

Many times our efforts are spent trying to help someone else, support a cause, assist a loved one, support a group and then you find yourself depleted without hope, depressed, sad or feeling empty…it is because you forgot along the way of helping others that **"YOU" are the mission!!**
Don't forget to care and love yourself!

*Follow @lifeimpactcc on FaceBook and Instragram for Quotes for Change!

References

AA History (1992). "The Origin of the Serenity Prayer" Retrieved from http://www.aahistory.com/prayer.html

"Children and Teens: Statistics" (2019) Retrieved from https://www.rainn.org/statistics/children-and-teens.

Community Tool Box, 2019. "Vision" Retrieved from https://ctb.ku.edu/en/search/node/vision%20statement

Diamond, S.A. (2008). This is an excerpt from Dr. Diamond's forthcoming book *Psychotherapy for the Soul: Thirty-Three Essential Secrets for Emotional and Spiritual Self-Healing.* Retrieved from https://www.psychologytoday.com/us/blog/evil-deeds/200806/essential-secrets-psychotherapy-the-inner-child

Gordan, D. (2013) "Coping Mechanism" Retrieved from http://magazine.ucla.edu/depts/lifesigns/coping-mechanism/

John Hopkins Medicine (2019). "Forgiveness Your Health Depends On It" Retrieved from https://www.hopkinsmedicine.org/health/wellness-and-prevention/forgiveness-your-health-depends-on-it

Mellody, P., Miller, A., J. K. Miller (2003). *Facing Codependency: What It Is, Where It Comes From, How It Sabotages Lives*. Harper: San Francisco

Merriam Dictionary (2016) Trauma. Retrieved from https://www.merriam-webster.com/dictionary/trauma

Merriam Dictionary (2019) Purposeful. Retrieved from https://www.merriam-webster.com/dictionary/purposeful

Merriam Dictionary (2019) Retrieved from https://www.merriam-webster.com/dictionary/anger

Merriam Dictionary (2019) Retrieved from https://www.merriam-webster.com/dictionary/honor

Merriam Dictionary (2019) Retrieved from https://www.merriam-webster.com/dictionary/value

Mulder, P. (2018). "Emotion Wheel by Robert Plutchik". Retrieved from Tools Hero: https://www.toolshero.com/psychology/personalhappiness/emotion-wheel-robert-plutchik/

Oxford Online Dictionary (2018) Victim. Retrieved from https://en.oxforddictionaries.com/definition/victim

Semel Institute for Neuroscience and Human Behavior (2018) "How Do You Cope." Retrieved from http://www2.semel.ucla.edu/dual-diagnosis-program/News_and_Resources/How_Do_You_Cope

Subramanian, S., Francis, R. D. (2012). The efficacy of an intervention on healing the inner child on emotional intelligence, and adjustment among the college students. *Indian Journal of Health and Wellbeing*. 3(3)., p. 648-652

Vivian, C. (2010). Putting Biblical Principles in Practice. (Personal communication, December 2017)

Wong, C. (2019). "How to Practice Mindfulness Meditation?" Retrieved from https://www.verywellmind.com/mindfulness-meditation-88369

University of North Carolina at Charlotte (2014). "Post-Traumatic Growth Research Group. What is PTG?" Retrieved from https://ptgi.uncc.edu/what-is-ptg/.

Conti, B. (1977) "Gonna Fly Now." Retrieved from https://genius.com/Bill-conti-gonna-fly-now-lyrics.

Miedaner, T. (2008). *The Secrets Laws of Attraction.* McGraw Hill: New York

Index

Abuse, VII, 6, 7, 8, 13, 14, 17, 36, 37
Abuse Cycle, 37, 89, 90, 91, 93
Acceptance, 6, 8, 9, 19, 37, 49-56, 68, 72-79, 82
Acceptance Chart, 56, 102

Anger, 86-90
Acknowledgment Chart, 54, 102
Childhood, 5, 8, 14, 16, 21-26, 29
Coping, 24-40, 86
Default Programming, 22, 25, 89, 94, 124, 130, 133, 136
Emotions, 12, 13, 14, 16, 87, 126
Emotion Wheel, 35, 45
Forgiveness, 54, 56, 71, 73, 77-101

Guilt, 46-71, 76, 87-94, 106
Healing, 38-39, 59, 109, 112, 135-136

Avoidant Coping, 27-30, 33, 85, 129
Active Coping, 27-30, 22, 85, 129
Journaling, 32, 120, 130

Meditation, 32-40, 69, 105, 118, 133
Mindfulness, 32, 75, 112, 137
Unhealthy Relationships
Purposeful, 19
Trauma, 12-14, 21-26
Inner Child, 27-30, 34, 85, 129-130
Internal Punishment, 123

Self-Acceptance, 49, 52, 109, 110, 126
Self-Love, 37, 39, 46, 49, 113, 126
Vision, 128-131

Inner Child, 27-30, 34, 85, 129-130

The Four A's Principle, 50, 78, 126, 129, 140

About the Author

Dr. Lisa Cook is a Licensed Professional Counselor, a Certified Professional Life Coach, and Co-Owner and Founder of Life Impact Circles Coaching Services. She has helped countless people to create life impact with relationships, pursue career aspirations, and grow personally through trauma recovery, counseling, coaching, and mentoring. She has been a Christian Education Instructor, Women's Conference and Retreat Speaker, Seminar Facilitator and Trainer.

She completed her Doctoral Research on "HIV Stigma Reduction and Health Literacy Education Program with a Cross Generational Population in an African American Faith-based Church". Her research is a model for the church context and public health structure to form partnerships to address barriers to health outcomes for underserved populations. Her research article is published in the Journal of Public Health.

Dr. Cook touts that of her greatest accomplishments is being a mother and a business partner with her daughter, Cieyara Porch, the two birthed Life Impact Circles in 2018. Life Impact Circles offers coaching to strengthen individuals to create the relationships that they deserve and seminars focusing on "Becoming Your Best Self" or "Mother/Daughter Relationships".

Professionally, Dr. Cook is currently employed as a Regional Operations Director for a managed care organization. She has 20+ years in behavioral, community and public health and she has had the pleasure to serve at-risk populations ranging from vulnerable children/youth with severely mental illness to seniors suffering with co-morbidities. She continues to strive for excellence as a volunteer at various non-for profit organizations.

www.ingramcontent.com/pod-product-compliance
Lightning Source LLC
Chambersburg PA
CBHW030325080526
44584CB00012B/722